THE WORLD OF 1 CORINTHIANS

Full-size colour versions of the photos and diagrams that appear in this book can be found at the companion website

www.worldof1corinthians.com

These are freely available for use in classrooms and churches.

THE WORLD OF 1 CORINTHIANS

An Exegetical Source Book of Literary and Visual Backgrounds

MATTHEW R. MALCOLM

CASCADE *Books* • Eugene, Oregon

THE WORLD OF 1 CORINTHIANS
An Exegetical Source Book of Literary and Visual Backgrounds

First published in Great Britain in 2012 by Paternoster, 52 Presley Way, Crownhill MK8 0ES. First US edition published by Cascade Books under license from Paternoster, 2011. US edition published by Cascade Books under license from Paternoster, 2013.

Cascade Books
An imprint of Wipf and Stock Publishers
199 W. 8th Ave., Suite 3
Eugene, OR 97401

www.wipfandstock.com

ISBN 13: 978-1-62032-983-2

Cataloging-in-Publication data:

Malcolm, Matthew R.

The world of 1 Corinthians : an exegetical source book of literary and visual backgrounds / Matthew R. Malcolm.

xliv + 170 p. ; 23 cm. Includes bibliographical references and index.

ISBN 13: 978-1-62032-983-2

1. Bible. N.T. Corinthians, 1st—Criticism, interpretation, etc. . 2. Bible. N.T.—Textbooks. I. Title.

BS2675.52 M142 2013

Manufactured in the U.S.A.
Typeset by Paternoster, UK

Contents

Preface

Interpreting an ancient biblical text involves recognising both the distance and the connection between the text and the reader. In terms of 1 Corinthians, this means that both the *historical background* and the *history of reception* of the letter are immensely important. This book represents an attempt to increase the 21st century reader's familiarity with the historical background of the letter.[1]

In recent decades, 1 Corinthians has perhaps received more investigation and speculation regarding historical backgrounds than any other biblical book. I do not intend to represent all of these investigations here. Rather, I seek to introduce the material, literary, cultural and conceptual settings that, in my opinion, are especially useful in illuminating the world in which the letter arose. Some of the sources that I include are relevant by way of contributing to a broad picture of the cultures involved, such as literature that evidences Roman conventions of honour and shame. Some of the sources indicate places or objects relevant to certain parts of the letter, such as depictions of hairstyle or descriptions of the Corinthian marketplace. Some sources are included in order to illustrate the uniqueness of Paul's approach, and others are included to show how similar he can be to other writers or traditions. A number of sources are included not because I am convinced of their definite interpretative value, but because they provide *possible* backgrounds to particular topics, such as the mystery cult of Eleusis. And some sources should be thought of as directly influential on the letter, such as the Old Testament motif of wilderness grumbling.

I present these sources with my own interpretative comments; and indeed this work should be thought of as a minimalist commentary of

---

1 For the early interpretation history of 1 Corinthians, see: Gerald Bray (ed), *Ancient Christian Commentary on Scripture: New Testament VII: 1–2 Corinthians* (Downers Grove, InterVarsity Press, 1999); and Judith L. Kovacs (ed), *1 Corinthians Interpreted by Early Christian Commentators* (Grand Rapids, Michigan, Eerdmans, 2005).

sorts, representing my own selection and analysis of relevant backgrounds. It will become evident that I view the most significant background of 1 Corinthians to be the Old Testament, but that I also find Jewish literature, Greco-Roman literature, and visual depictions to be of enormous value in illuminating the letter.

One area that is of particular interest to me is the arrangement of 1 Corinthians, an issue that I think can be very fruitfully investigated in the light of the backgrounds mentioned above. For this reason I provide an overview of this topic in the introduction, and give extra discussion of relevant texts in three excurses:

1) Chapters 1–4 and Reversal
2) Chapters 5–14 and Pauline Ethics
3) Chapter 15 and Reversal

In these sections I adapt some material from my dissertation (Cambridge University Press, forthcoming). The book can be profitably used whether or not one agrees with my assessment of the letter's arrangement, but I hope to provoke fresh consideration of this significant issue.

In this work I assume the Pauline authorship of the letter (with Sosthenes), in 53 – 55 CE, as a unified composition. Where I have found secondary sources to be particularly helpful in dealing with specific backgrounds I have referred to them in footnotes. I have also used footnotes to provide a sense of the context of each citation of ancient literature. I have only provided full citations of Old Testament passages where the distinctiveness of the Septuagint is instructive.

In terms of terminology for cultures and periods, I have made use of broad categories that carry the danger of being misunderstood. It would be wrong to infer from my terminology that Jewish, Greek and Roman cultures were neatly separable. On the other hand, however, it would also be wrong to think of the cultural distinctives of Judaism as having been swallowed up and dissolved in Greek or Roman culture. Therefore I retain the broad categories but suggest that the reader interpret the references with this caution in mind.

I wish to thank a number of people for helping with this project. Anthony Thiselton has been an inspiration on 1 Corinthians and a great encourager. I am thankful for his vast knowledge and humble friendship. I am grateful to Roland Deines for providing pictures of Ephesus and Jerusalem and for enlarging my appreciation of early Judaism. Christoph Ochs helped greatly with producing the reconstruction of the Temple of Apollo, while Morgana Wingard and Andrew and Bethany Talbert assisted with adjusting the maps. Peter Watts painstakingly proofread my text and helped with Greek fonts. My parents Ian and Kaye also read through the work and provided helpful feedback. I am warmly grateful for all of these contributions.

Part of the preparation for this book occurred in Greece as my wife and children accompanied me on a trip to the various locations pictured in the book. On our first day we suffered a rather serious car accident, and although we were all safe, my wife Rebecca spent the rest of our time in Greece with two black eyes. Nevertheless she continued to enjoy the trip, and later cheerfully helped with background research for the book. I dedicate this book to her, with great affection.

Introduction

Orientation to the Backgrounds of 1 Corinthians

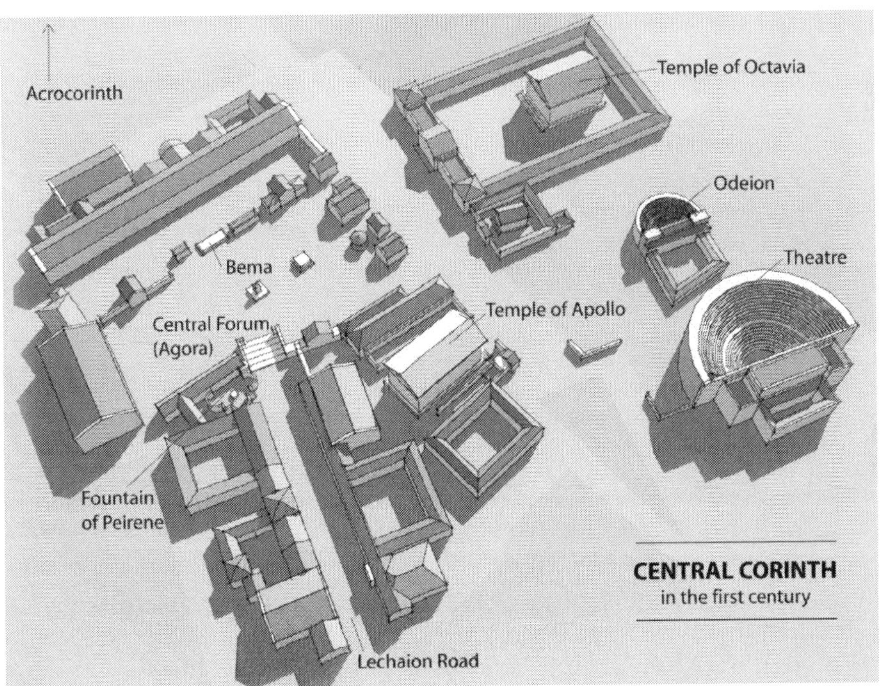

Locations

When Paul wrote to "the church of God that is in Corinth" he was writing to a large and strategically-placed Roman colony. The city had been destroyed by the Roman general Mummius in 146 BCE, and, after being left desolate, colonised by Julius Caesar in 44 BCE. The temple of Apollo was retained from the Greek era, and the city continued to participate in the pan-Hellenic games; but it quickly became a busy centre that was thoroughly Roman in character.

The importance of Corinth as a city was partly due to geography. It was situated between the harbours of Lechaion on the North and Cenchreae on the South-East. It also linked mainland Greece on the East with the Peloponnese on the West. This location provided Corinth with a unique and busy emporium.

Within the city of Roman Corinth were numerous temples and shrines, a central *agora* or *forum*, shops, fountains, and theatres. The remains, and their descriptions in literature, illuminate themes in 1 Corinthians such as the imagery of the theatre, the sale of meat at the marketplace, and the Corinthian esteem of wealth.

See comments, citations and pictures relating to:

1:2 (site of ancient Corinth)
1:12–16 (fountains of Glauke and Peirene, Gulf of Corinth, location of Corinth between seas)
1:26 (location on the Isthmus)
2:1 (*diolkos*, Lechaion Road, temple of Apollo, temple of Octavia; description of the *agora*)
3:9 (fields surrounding Corinth)
4:9 (theatres)
6:4 (*bema*)
8:9 (temple of Apollo, Acrocorinth)
10:25 (*agora*, shops, Lechaion Road, town plan)
15:6 (description of road to Corinth)

Other locations are also important for 1 Corinthians. When Paul first visited Corinth he had come from Athens (where, according to Acts, he engaged with Stoic and Epicurean philosophers), and presumably passed through Eleusis (which was a major Greek religious centre). At the time that 1 Corinthians was written Paul was in Ephesus, and expected that he would soon return to Corinth before bringing financial help to Christians in Jerusalem. Rome, although not mentioned in 1 Corinthians, remained influential on its Corinthian colony.

See comments, citations and pictures relating to:

2:1 (Athens, Eleusis, map showing Athens, Eleusis and Corinth)
2:6 (Eleusis)
3:9 (Jerusalem temple)
4:9 (Arch of Titus in Rome)
9:24 (Nemea, Isthmia, map showing Corinth, Nemea and Isthmia)
15:32 (theatre in Ephesus, Colosseum in Rome)
16:19 (map showing Corinth and Ephesus)

Artefacts

There are numerous artefacts and materials in the region of ancient Corinth that help illuminate elements of 1 Corinthians. Statues, gravestones, inscriptions and artwork give insights into values, customs, and assumptions. Statues and portraiture indicate conventions of dress, head covering and banqueting, and inscriptions such as the Erastus pavement or Babbius monument express conventions of honour and reciprocity.

See comments and pictures relating to:

1:12–16 (water supply)
1:26 (Babbius monument)
2:1 (Erastus pavement)
4:9 (theatre decoration)
6:13 (Aphrodite with nymphs)
8:10 (depictions of banqueting on grave decorations)
11:4 (bust of Nero)

Similar artefacts from other regions also provide useful illumination. Gravestones point to attitudes toward death, Roman coins illustrate Roman values, writing materials illustrate conventions of written communication, and religious objects convey conventions such as sacrifice and priesthood.

See comments and pictures relating to:

2:1 (artwork depicting Eleusinian mysteries; bust of Demeter)
2:6 (Eleusinian telesterion, depiction of mysteries)
2:8 (coins of Claudius and Nero; statues of Claudius and Nero)
5:9 (stylus and reproduction wax tablets)
6:13 (depictions of the body in Greco-Roman art and sculpture, including Aphrodite)
9:1 (coin of Claudius depicting Libertas)
9:24 (prize base from Greek games)
10:18 (sacrificial eschara)
10:25 (statue of Ephesian Artemis; statue of Dionysus; mosaic of Dionysus)
11:4 (statues of Roman emperors with headcoverings)
11:5 (depictions of Greco-Roman women's headcoverings)
11:21 (internal decoration in a Roman house)
12:14 (bust of Asklepios)
15:6 (Greek tombstones)
15:32 (Ephesian theatre; Roman Colosseum)

Literary and Rhetorical Features

A number of the quotations from ancient literature in this volume illustrate the ways in which other writers employ similar – or contrasting – literary devices. These include *epistolary features*, such as employing secretaries, utilising conventional greetings and thanksgivings, and ending with the author's own handwriting; *rhetorical features*, such as structures of argumentation, digression, and "metaschematismos"; and utilisation of *common topics*, phrases and words that enlighten similar motifs in 1 Corinthians.

Aside from biblical quotations and allusions (which can be found in the index), see comments and citations relating to:

1:1 (co-senders of letters)
1:3 (greetings)
1:4 (thanksgiving)
1:10–11 (the topics of zeal and strife)
1:12 (language of belonging)
3:1 (metaphor of infancy)
3:10 (metaphor of laying a foundation)
4:6 (rhetorical device of *metaschematismos*)
4:16 (motif of imitation)
Excursus 5–14 (ordering of ethical sections)
5:9 (ancient letter writing)
6:1 (*parekbasis*: rhetorical digression)
7:9 (image of burning for sexual desire)
9:3 (digression; the language of defence)
9:19–22 (images of adaptability)
9:25 (imagery of training)
10:1 (motif of the wilderness cloud)
10:11 (example and exhortation)
11:17 (digression)
12:12, 15, 21, 26 (metaphor of the multi-membered body)
12:31 (interlude)
13:1 (verse)
13:11 (imagery of childhood and maturity)
13:12 (image of the mirror)
14:9, 11 (motif of unclear communication)
15:1 (Greco-Roman rhetorical organisation)
15:4 (motif of the third day)
15:32 (metaphor of beasts)
15:33 (proverb from Menander)

15:50 (term "flesh and blood")
15:53 (terms "perishability" and "immortality")
15:57 (common phrase)
16:21 (handwritten confirmation)

Customs and Rituals

In addition to the pictures listed above, many of the ancient authors shed light on customs such as hairstyle, clothing, eating, and oratory; and rituals such as sacrifice and cult meals. These provide some illumination of issues in 1 Corinthians such as common meals, headcoverings and quarrelling over "wise speech".

See comments and citations relating to:
1:12 (leadership)
1:14 (baptism)
1:17 (philosophy, oratory, sophistry)
1:22 (Greek pursuit of wisdom)
1:23 (crucifixion)
2:1 (Eleusinian mysteries)
3:5 (benefits and reciprocity)
4:2 (stewards)
4:9 (gladiatorial fights; Roman victories)
4:10 (Greek theatre)
4:15 (instructors)
5:1 (marriage laws and customs)
5:2 (benefaction)
6:4 (lawsuits)
6:5–8 (public courts and internal justice)
6:20 (slavery and ownership)
7:10 (Roman and Jewish laws and customs regarding divorce)
7:18 (circumcision and its removal)
7:21 (slavery and freedom)
7:32 (Stoic conception of marriage)
7:36–8 (virgins)
8:4 (meat sacrificed to idols)
8:9 (invitations to cult meals)
9:6 (benefaction and oratory)
9:15 (Greek "rights")
9:25 (games and wreaths)
11:4 (Roman men's headcoverings)

11:5 (women's hair and headcoverings)
11:21 (customs of dining)
11:33 (community in religious rites)
12:3 (Corinthian curse tablets)
14:4 (speaking in tongues)
14:15 (ecstatic prophecy)
14:23 (ecstatic religious behaviour)
14:32 (prophecy)
14:35 (Roman conventions of marriage)

Concepts and Beliefs

Perhaps the most significant insights provided by the ancient literature in this volume concern Jewish, Greek, and Roman cultural conceptualisations. These include pervasive assumptions and beliefs such as Old Testament conceptions of divinity and worship, Jewish expectations of divinely granted reversal, Greco-Roman values of honour and benefaction, and varying beliefs about bodies, souls and the afterlife.

Aside from biblical quotations and allusions (which can be found in the index), see comments and citations relating to:

Excursus 1–4 (Jewish motif of double reversal)
1:19 (Jewish motif of double reversal)
1:26 (Roman status and values; conceptions of good fortune; conceptions of power and nobility)
1:30 (Jewish and Roman conceptions of boasting)
2:6 (Eleusinian mysteries; Jewish apocalyptic)
2:8 (Jewish conception of the boastful ruler; apocalyptic distinction between the ages; distinction between human and divine)
2:13 (Stoic and Jewish concepts of the Spirit; distinction between human and divine)
3:4 (Jewish distinction between human and divine; boasting)
3:9–10, 16 (Jewish concept of community as temple)
3:13 (Stoic belief in final conflagration; Jewish ideas of testing by fire)
3:18 (Jewish apocalyptic eschatology)
4:5 (Roman and Stoic conventions of honour and praise)
4:10 (Greco-Roman regard for honour)
4:16 (value of imitation)
Excursus 5–14 (Greco-Roman and Jewish conceptions of morality)
5:7 (Jewish theme of purity and impurity)
6:3 (Jewish belief in future communal judgement)

6:5 (Roman conventions of honour and shame)
6:12 (Roman conceptions of freedom and authority)
6:13 (Greek concept of noble desire)
6:15 (Stoic concept of God in the individual)
7:1 (Roman and Jewish conceptions of marriage and pleasure)
7:14 (illegitimacy and moral impurity)
7:26 (apocalyptic crisis)
7:32 (Cynic asceticism)
8:4 (Jewish monotheism and idols)
8:9 (offending Jewish sensibilities)
9:15 (Stoic acceptance)
9:22 (Jewish concept of divine accommodation)
11:10 (angelic watchers)
11:14 (Jewish and Roman views of nature)
Excursus 15 (Jewish motif of double reversal)
15:6 (Roman considerations of death)
15:10 (Roman and Jewish views of labour)
15:19 (pursuit of present pleasure)
15:21 (Jewish problem of death)
15:25–27 (Jewish motif of double reversal)
15:31 (Stoic consideration of death)
15:35 (Greek, Roman, and Jewish views of the soul and the body)
15:37 (Stoic interest in astrology)
15:45 (Jewish beliefs in creation and resurrection)
15:53 (Epicurean and Jewish conceptions of immortality)
15:55 (Jewish personification of death)
15:57 (Jewish motif of double reversal)

Content and Arrangement of 1 Corinthians

The question of a central theme in 1 Corinthians is closely linked to the question of the arrangement of the letter. However, the arrangement of 1 Corinthians is a topic on which there is no present consensus. Especially since Johannes Weiss, some have suggested that because of literary incongruities and a lack of overall coherence, it is best viewed as an *Edited Collection* of letters,[1] although this view is not as prominent as it once was.

[1] See Johannes Weiss, *Der Erste Korintherbrief* (Göttingen, Vandenhoeck & Ruprecht, 1925). For a recent adherent of this view see L.L. Welborn, *Paul, the Fool of Christ: A Study of 1 Corinthians 1 – 4 in the Comic-Philosophic Tradition* (London, T&T Clark, 2005).

Linda Belleville argues that *Epistolary Analysis* sheds light on the flow of the letter,[2] but this has proven to be most helpful for the beginning and ending of the letter, rather than the substance of the main body.

More recently, Rhetorical Criticism has arisen as a tool for analysing Pauline letters. Broadly, this development aims to do justice to Pauline texts as *argumentation*. Specifically, *Rhetorical Criticism* very often seeks to understand Pauline argumentation in the light of patterns of *speech rhetoric* seen in handbooks and textual examples of the Aristotelian tradition. The most influential application to 1 Corinthians is by Margaret M. Mitchell, who argues that the letter ought to be seen as a "merging" of the letter genre with the conventions of Greco-Roman speech rhetoric. 1 Corinthians, she argues, is an example of "deliberative rhetoric", and can consequently be interpreted in the light of the conventions and intentions of this genre. If this is the case, Mitchell contends, the letter must be an extended exhortation to pursue *congregational unity*. However it would seem that, although it is unquestionably useful to analyse Pauline letters in terms of the movement of their lengthy argumentation, there is no certainty that New Testament letter-writers intentionally made use of the conventions of speech-rhetoric in considering macro-structure – or that the issue of congregational unity lies behind each topic of the letter.[3]

J.C. Hurd interacts to some degree with Epistolary Analysis, but hints that formal conventions are subject to a more fundamental determiner of structure in 1 Corinthians, Paul's *Pastoral Strategy*:[4] Hurd sees Paul as being literarily creative in inventing or employing textual patterns that serve his pastoral purposes, despite perhaps appearing at first to involve

---

[2] Linda L. Belleville, "Continuity or Discontinuity: A Fresh Look at 1 Corinthians in the Light of First-Century Epistolary Forms and Conventions" *Evangelical Quarterly* LIX/1 (1987), 15–37.

[3] Ben Witherington III, who detects Greco-Roman rhetorical convention in the structure of Pauline letters, concedes: "Most New Testament scholars at this juncture are convinced that micro-rhetoric (that is, rhetorical devices such as rhetorical questions, dramatic hyperbole or personification) can be found in the New Testament documents, particularly in Paul's letters, but also elsewhere. More controversial is whether macro-rhetoric (whether the overall structure of the document reflects rhetorical categories and divisions) is also used in the New Testament." Ben Witherington III, "Rhetorical Criticism" in Paula Gooder (ed), *Searching for Meaning: An Introduction to Interpreting the New Testament* (London, SPCK, 2008, 2009), 72.

[4] John C. Hurd, "Good News and the Integrity of 1 Corinthians" in Jervis & Richardson (eds), *Gospel in Paul: Studies in 1 Corinthians, Galatians and Romans* (Sheffield, Sheffield Academic Press, 1994).

literary incongruities such as unnecessary repetition. Hurd's particular view of the arrangement of the letter has not received broad acceptance, but this insight is useful. John Calvin had similarly dealt with the apparently incongruous placement of chapter 15 by appealing to a sort of creative "pastoral" rhetoric.[5]

Paul's rhetoric is sometimes conceived as responding to a set of problems in Corinth that itself exhibits a unifying coherence. Once this (entextualised) *Situational Coherence* is recognised, apparent inconsistencies in literary flow (either of the whole letter or of a section) may become less troublesome. Such situational coherence has been characterised variously in terms of:

a. Primarily problematic beliefs (*Gnostic or mystery religiosity* according to Helmut Koester;[6] *over-realised eschatology* or *pneumatistic premature triumphalism* according to Anthony C. Thiselton;[7] competing conceptions of *wisdom* according to James A. Davis[8] and David R. Hall[9])

---

[5] John Calvin, *Commentary on the Epistles of Paul the Apostle to the Corinthians*, Vol. 1. (Grand Rapids, Michigan, Baker, 1979), 7–8.

[6] "The entire polemic of 1 Corinthians must be seen as an argument against understanding the new message about Jesus as a mystery religion, and as a plea for understanding the "new existence" as entrance into the community of the new age." "The Silence of the Apostle" in Schowalter, Daniel N. & Friesen, Steven J. (eds), *Urban Religion in Roman Corinth: Interdisciplinary Approaches* (Cambridge, Massachusetts, Harvard University Press), 346.

[7] See especially Anthony C. Thiselton, "Realized Eschatology at Corinth" *New Testament Studies* 24 (1978), 510–526; and *The First Epistle to the Corinthians* (Grand Rapids, Michigan, Eerdmans, 2000).

[8] "The central issue of the letter would be the one highlighted within this opening section, namely, the issue of deciding upon the locus, content, source and purpose of the wisdom which would guide the community and the individuals within it into proper sorts of Christian behaviour. What sort of wisdom was to govern their morality, their response to food that had been dedicated to idols, the conduct of their worship, and the shape of their hope for the resurrection?" James A. Davis, *Wisdom and Spirit: An Investigation of 1 Corinthians 1:18–3:20 Against the Background of Jewish Sapiential Traditions in the Greco-Roman Period* (Lanham, MD, University Press of America, 1984), 145.

[9] "Paul regards the 'wisdom' criticized in chs. 1–4 as a common feature of all the parties, and when discussing the behavioural problems resulting from that 'wisdom' in chs. 5–16, addresses his remarks to the church as a whole." David R. Hall, *The Unity of the Corinthian Correspondence* (London, T&T Clark, 2003), 30.

b. Primarily problematic behaviour (*disunity* according to Mitchell;[10] secular-inspired *conflict and compromise* according to Bruce Winter;[11] *elitism* according to Gerd Theissen;[12] *social distinctions* according to David G. Horrell;[13] *rhetorical competitiveness* according to Duane Litfin)[14]

Of course, these varying characterisations of a unified set of problems in Corinth need not be seen as utterly incompatible with one another. Indeed it may be observed that there is a degree of agreement that the problems in Corinth involved community conflict in combination with exclusivistic and worldly religiosity. Such characterisations of entextualised situational coherence may prove fruitful in alleviating literary incongruities, and so ought to be attended to in the consideration of exegetical tensions within 1 Corinthians.

Certain scholars maintain that, in connection with his conception of the problems in Corinth, Paul exhibits a *Unifying Theological Thesis* that directs his creative pastoral strategy. Such scholars do not generally deny that social and religious factors fruitfully illuminate the Corinthian situation to which Paul responds, but they see in Paul's response a theological theme that is more

---

10 "1 Corinthians is a unified deliberative letter which throughout urges unity on the divided Corinthian church." Mitchell, *Paul and the Rhetoric*, 296.

11 See both: Bruce W. Winter, *After Paul Left Corinth: The Influence of Secular Ethics and Social Change* (Grand Rapids, Michigan/Cambridge, Eerdmans, 2001); and "The 'Underlays' of Conflict and Compromise in 1 Corinthians" in Burke, Trevor J. & Elliott, J. Keith (eds), *Paul and the Corinthians: Studies on a Community in Conflict* (Leiden/Boston, Brill, 2003), 139–155.

12 "[T]he Corinthian congregation is marked by internal stratification. The majority of the members, who come from the lower classes, stand in contrast to a few influential members who come from the upper classes." Gerd Theissen, *The Social Setting of Pauline Christianity* (Edinburgh, T&T Clark, 1982), 69.

13 "Having outlined the social diversity encompassed within the Corinthian community, I now seek to outline a number of situations revealed in 1 Corinthians in which there is some evidence that social distinctions or social factors play a part in creating the problems which Paul addresses. This is not to deny that sociological factors may have played some role in other aspects of the church's life which Paul addresses, nor that theological factors are also bound up in the situations of social tension and conflict." David G. Horrell, *The Social Ethos of the Corinthian Correspondence: Interests and Ideology from 1 Corinthians to 1 Clement* (Edinburgh, T&T Clark, 1996), 101.

14 See Duane Litfin, *St. Paul's Theology of Proclamation: 1 Corinthians 1 – 4 and Greco–Roman Rhetoric* (Cambridge, Cambridge University Press, 1994).

fundamental for the arrangement of the letter. Thus both the framing of the Corinthian problems and the organisation of Paul's response are to be understood as evidencing a theologically driven rhetoric. This is not to say that those in Corinth consciously held theological views divergent from those of the apostle; rather, the apostle perceives that the Corinthians' religious and social problems are manifestations of a deeper theological problem, and so he responds with a letter that is organised in such a way as to present a primarily theological correction. So Karl Barth characterises the core problem as "unrestrained human vitality", a theological issue that expresses itself in different ways throughout the letter until it is climactically answered in chapter 15: Humans should place their confidence in the *God* who raises the dead – and this should be demonstrated in their religious beliefs and behaviours.[15] David A. Ackerman argues that Paul's theological conception of Corinthian problems is best thought of as "spiritual immaturity", and that Paul's centrally theological response can be fruitfully summed up as "Christ-ideology".[16]

It is certainly worthy of note that canonical 1 Corinthians begins with an extended reflection on the significance of the cross, and ends with an extended reflection on the significance of resurrection. These Christological events are both described as constitutive of Paul's "gospel", initially received by the Corinthians with "faith", but since endangered by possible retreat into "vanity". These striking echoes may be reason enough to take seriously attempts to detect a fundamental theological unity in the letter.[17]

A few Pauline scholars have explored the possibility that Paul employs patterns of *Rhetorical Formulation from his Theological Heritage* (particularly the Old Testament and early Judaism) in order to give shape to a unified theological force in his letter. Ciampa and Rosner posit a resonance with the ethical concerns of Second Temple Judaism (in particular, the "Gentile" problems of sexual immorality and idolatry),[18] resulting in

---

15 Karl Barth, *The Resurrection of the Dead*, Trans H.J. Stenning (Eugene, Oregon, Wipf & Stock Publishers, 2003).

16 David A. Ackerman, *Lo, I Tell You a Mystery: Cross, Resurrection, and Paraenesis in the Rhetoric of 1 Corinthians* (Eugene, Oregon, Pickwick Publications, 2006), 24.

17 Grayston comments: "Thus, whether by design or accident, the epistle is constructed as a development and qualification of the early formula 'Christ died and rose again'." Kenneth Grayston, *Dying, We Live: A New Inquiry into the Death of Christ in the New Testament* (Darton, Longman and Todd, 1990), 16.

18 "It is widely recognized that in early Jewish and Christian thinking Gentiles were consistently characterized by two particularly abhorrent vices: sexual immorality and idolatry." Roy E. Ciampa and Brian S. Rosner, "The Structure and Argument of 1 Corinthians: A Biblical/Jewish Approach" *New Testament Studies* 52 (2006), 205–218; 207.

an understandable theologically-driven appeal for holiness in response to Corinthian worldliness:

I. Letter Opening (1:1–9)
II. True and False Wisdom and Corinthian Factionalism (1:10–4:17)
III. "Flee Sexual Immorality" [and Greed] and "Glorify God with your Bodies" (4:18–7:40)
IV. "Flee Idolatry" and "Glorify God" in Your Worship (8:1–14:40)
V. The Resurrection and Consummation (15:1–58)
VI. Letter Closing (16:1–24)[19]

A similar pattern of argumentation is said to exist in other Pauline letters. Indeed, attentiveness to possible parallel patterns of argumentation across Paul and in his conscious theological heritage suggests itself as a worthy pursuit.

Michael J. Gorman likewise sees a theological coherence in 1 Corinthians that is expressed in rhetorical patterns from Paul's theological heritage (specifically, patterns of reversal). Gorman views chapters 1–4 as focusing on the cross; 5–7 as exploring moral consequences; 8–14 as exploring liturgical consequences; and chapter 15 as presenting the reversal of the cross in resurrection.[20]

The arrangement of 1 Corinthians that I present in this book is in continuity with these latter directions, and especially seeks to be attentive to important elements of the letter's original "world". Two features are worth noting:

1. The Jewish motif of (double) reversal

I suggest that Paul (with Sosthenes) draws on the conceptual motif of the *condemned boaster* and the *vindicated sufferer*, seen in the Psalms and prophets (such as Psalm 2 and Daniel 1–6), developed in early Jewish writings (such as the *Wisdom of Solomon* and the *Epistle of Enoch*), and utilised significantly in early Christian reception of Jesus (such as Mark's Gospel and Acts).

In this light, I suggest that 1 Corinthians confronts the Corinthians with a choice: Will they align themselves with those who boastfully scorn the

[19] Abridged from Ciampa and Rosner, *Structure and Argument*, 212–213. See also Eckhard J. Schnabel, *Der Erste Brief des Paulus an die Korinther* (Wuppertal, Brockhaus, 2006), 48–9, for a similar structure.

[20] Michael J. Gorman, *Apostle of the Crucified Lord: A Theological Introduction to Paul and His Letters* (Grand Rapids, Michigan, Eerdmans, 2004).

dead – the "rulers of this age" who "crucified the Lord of glory" – or will they become imitators of Christ's apostles who "have been condemned to death" and "die every day"? Will they assume the role of the *boaster who awaits condemnation*, or the *sufferer who awaits vindication*?

Thus, chapters 1–4 emphasise the *cross of Christ*, in distinction to boastful and divisive notions of spirituality and leadership in Roman Corinth. Chapters 5–14 relate this cruciform corrective to a series of ethical issues (see below). Chapter 15 returns to the themes and terminology of chapters 1–4, insisting that the *resurrection of Christ* brings assurance of the future condemnation of the rulers of this age, and the future vindication of the dead.

2. *The flow of Pauline ethics*

I suggest that the main ethical section of the letter (chapters 5–14) applies Paul's emphasis on dependence on God's crucified Messiah to an observable pattern of topics for a Pauline ethical section. As in other Pauline letters, the congregation is firstly called to sanctification in relation to the fundamental issues of sexual immorality, greed, and impurity of bodies (chapters 5–7). Secondly, the congregation is called to sanctification in relation to interactional issues within the body of Christ (chapters 8–14). This flow of issues also echoes the ethics of other Jewish writings of the Hellenistic-Roman eras.

As a whole, then, the letter summons the Christians of Corinth into the narrative of Christ's own passion, calling them to share in his death in the present, apply it to the behavioural problems arising in the context of Roman Corinth, and to look ahead to sharing in Christ's resurrected vindication in the future. This might be thought of as a flexible *Kerygmatic Rhetoric*.[21]

---

[21] The three excurses in this book will show the conceptual and literary backgrounds of such an arrangement. A more detailed argument can be found in my dissertation, *Kerygma in the Arrangement of 1 Corinthians: The Impact of Paul's Gospel on Paul's Macro-Rhetoric* (Cambridge University Press, forthcoming). For similar conceptions of a central theme, see Thiselton, *First Epistle*, 40: "The unifying theme of the epistle is a reproclamation of the different value system of grace, gifts, the cross, and the resurrection as divine verdict, criterion, and status bestowal within the new framework of respect and love for the less esteemed 'other'. Glorying in the Lord and receiving status derived from identification with the crucified Christ (1:30–31) lead to a new value system demonstrable in a wide array of life issues". Also, Gordon D. Fee, *The First Epistle to the Corinthians* (Grand Rapids, Michigan, Eerdmans, 1987), 16: "[H]ere Paul is doing what he does best, bringing the gospel to bear in the marketplace."

Structure in Brief:

1:1–9: Greetings and Thanksgiving
Chapters 1(:10)–4: The Cross Confronts Divisive Autonomous Boasting in Human Wisdom
 1:10–2:5: God's cross and human wisdom
 2:6–3:4: God's Spirit and human capability
 3:5–4:5: God's work and human authority
 4:6–21: God's (cruciform) way and human boasting

Chapters 5–7: The Cross Applied I: Your Body Belongs to the Lord
 5:1–7:40: Sexual immorality and greed

Chapters 8–14: The Cross Applied II: Discern the Body
 8:1–11:1: Knowledge and rights
 11:2–11:34: Tradition and division
 12:1–14:40: Gifts and love

Chapter 15: The Resurrection Condemns Earthly Powers and Vindicates the Dead
 15:1–58: Present death and future resurrection

Chapter 16: Those who labour

Structure in Detail:

1:1–9: Greetings and Thanksgiving

Chapters 1–4: The Cross Confronts Divisive Autonomous Boasting in Human Wisdom
God's cross and human wisdom
 1:10–12: Let there be unity rather than competitive division
 1:13–17: The apostolic task is not baptism but proclamation of the gospel – not in words of *human* wisdom
 1:18–25: *Human* wisdom fails before *God* – whose power is revealed in the cross
 1:26–31: One should not boast in *human status* but, through Christ, in God
 2:1–5: The basis for faith must not be human wisdom, but *God's* power, revealed in Christ crucified

God's Spirit and human capability

2:6–10: *Human rulers* fail to perceive the things of God; but God has revealed them to his own people by his Spirit

2:10–16: Those who lack *God's Spirit* lack understanding; but those who have God's Spirit have the mind of Christ

3:1–4: The Corinthians are not acting as *Spiritual* people, but as those who are proudly human

God's work and human authority

3:5–9: Paul and Apollos are co-workers of *God*

3:10–17: Those who build other than on the divinely-provided foundation will receive rejection by *God*

3:21–23: Boasting in *humans* has no place for those who are possessed by *God*

4:1–5: *Human* judgements about leaders are inconsequential; what matters is praise from *God*

God's (cruciform) way and human boasting

4:6–7: Those who receive from *God* are in no position to compete and boast

4:8–13: The Corinthians are mistakenly acting as those who reign; the apostles are acting as those who die

4:14–21: The Corinthians are to imitate Paul: The kingdom of *God* is not a matter of speech, but of power

Chapters 5–7: The Cross Applied I: Your Body Belongs to the Lord

Sexual Immorality and Greed

A: 5:1–13: Sexual Immorality (the refusal to judge)

B: 6:1–11: Greedy exploitation (an apparent inability to judge)

A^1: 6:12–7:40: Sexual Immorality, the body, marriage

Chapters 8–14: The Cross Applied II: Discern the Body

Knowledge and Rights

A: 8:1–13: Meat offered to idols (using knowledge and rights to endanger weaker brothers & sisters)

B: 9:1–27 Paul's example/defence (foregoing rights for others and self)

A^1: 10:1–11:1: Meat offered to idols (foregoing rights for self and others)

Tradition and Division

A: 11:2–16: "I praise you for keeping the traditions I passed on" (public worship)

B: 11:17–22: "I do *not* praise you" (in both v17 and v22)
A^{1}: 11:23–34: "I passed on to you what I also received" (tradition of Lord's Supper)

Gifts and Love

A: 12:1–31: Gifts within the body (mutual interdependence)
B: 12:31–13:13: Love
A^{1}: 14:1–40: Gifts (for ordered edification of the whole)

Chapter 15: The Resurrection Condemns Earthly Powers and Vindicates the Dead
Present Death and Future Resurrection

15:1–11: The gospel of the died and risen Christ, attested by witnesses who are marred by death
15:12–19: The Corinthian denial of "the resurrection of the dead" undermines apostolic witness and its effects
15:20–28, 29–34: Christ has been raised, initiating both the resurrection of the dead who belong to him (such as the apostles), and the abolition of rival rulers
15:35–49: While *humans* offer a dead, bare "seed" of a body in the present, the creator God will bring transformative Spiritual clothing in the future
15:50–57: All *human* ("flesh and blood") mortality must be clothed with divine immortality in *Christ*
15:58: This validates (cruciform) labour in the present

Chapter 16: Those Who Labour

16:1–4: Collection for Jerusalem
16:5–12: External figureheads: Paul, Timothy, Apollos
16:13–18: Church labourers: Stephanas, Fortunatus, Achaicus
16:19–24: Greetings

Ancient Literature and Authors

The Old Testament

The single most important background for understanding Paul is undoubtedly the Old Testament. Paul's Scriptures illuminate many of Paul's topics, including the nature of God, the identity and calling of God's people, the work of the Messiah, and the future. Perhaps the most relevant parts of the Old Testament are Genesis 1–3; the Pentateuchal wandering narratives; the Psalms; Isaiah; and Daniel. The Old Testament references can be found in the index.

Ancient Inscriptions and Papyrus Documents

There are various collections of ancient Greco-Roman inscriptions and documents, covering a range of genres and topics. These provide insights into the everyday concerns, values and customs of people of the New Testament era.

Useful Greek and Latin primary sources that I have consulted include:

New Documents Illustrating Early Christianity (Sydney, Macquarie University; ongoing series);

Neil Hopkinson (ed) *A Hellenistic Anthology* (Cambridge, University of Cambridge, 1988);

A.S. Hunt and C.C. Edgar, *Select Papyri: Private Affairs, With an English Translation*, Loeb Classical Library (Cambridge, Massachusetts, Harvard University Press, 1932);

John Harvey Kent, *Corinth Vol. VIII, Part III: The Inscriptions 1926–1950* (Princeton, New Jersey, The American School of Classical Studies at Athens, 1966);

Henry G. Meecham, *Light From Ancient Letters: Private Correspondence in the Nonliterary Papyri of Oxyrhynchus of the First Four Centuries, and its Bearing on New Testament Language and Thought* (Eugene, Oregon, Wipf & Stock Publishers, 1923);

Michael Trapp (ed), *Greek and Latin Letters: An Anthology with Translation* (Cambridge, Cambridge University Press, 2003);
A.B. West, *Corinth Vol. VIII, Part II: Latin Inscriptions 1896–1926* (Cambridge, Massachusetts, Harvard University Press, 1931);
The Packard Humanities Institute Greek Inscriptions: http://epigraphy.packhum.org/inscriptions/

See the citations relating to 1:3 (papyrus letter), 1:4 (papyrus letter); 1:17 (statue base inscription; imperial "gospel" inscription), 1:26 (base inscription); 2:1 (pavement inscription); 2:6 (statue base inscription); 4:2 (honorary inscription), 4:10 (honorary inscription); 5:1 (statue base); 6:5 (association rules); 7:10 (marriage contracts); 7:21 (slave manumission document); 8:9 (banquet invitations); 8:10 (statue inscription); 9:6 (papyrus letter); 11:17 (statue base inscriptions); 11:23–26, 28, 31 (association rules; song lyrics); 14:29–36 (association rules); 15:4 ("Gabriel Revelation"); 15:57 (papyrus letter); 16:3 (papyrus letter of recommendation); 16:21 (papyrus letter).

The Ancient Authors and their Works

Achilles Tatius

Achilles Tatius was a Greek novelist, possibly from Alexandria in the second century CE. His one surviving work is the romantic story *The Adventures of Leucippe and Clitophon*. The relevance to 1 Corinthians is simply in the terminology that he uses in speaking about virginity and hairstyle.
See comments relating to 7:36–38; 11:15.

Aeschines

Aeschines (c.390 – c.322 BCE) trained as an actor and fought as a soldier before his political career. He opposed Demosthenes and hoped that Philip of Macedon would bring about a united, peaceful Greece. However, he ended up in exile in Asia Minor and Rhodes, where he delivered speeches. Philostratus later considered Aeschines to have anticipated the revitalization of Greek rhetoric known as the Second Sophistic.

His relevance in this work is the way in which certain comments exemplify the interest in rights and self-defence that was characteristic of Greco-Roman culture over a wide period.

See comments relating to 9:15.

Aeschylus

Aeschylus (525/4 – 456/5 BCE) was the first great classical Greek dramatist. He is known especially for tragedies, and his work was influential on Greek drama and culture. His relevance to 1 Corinthians is very indirect: passing references to themes such as slavery illuminate a history behind their Roman manifestations.

See comments relating to 7:21; 14:9.

Antipater of Tarsus

Antipater of Tarsus (c.200 – 129 BCE) was a philosopher who led the Stoic school in Athens. His relevance in this volume is his work *On Marriage*, in which he advocates a positive vision of marriage. Marriage, Antipater urges, is an institution that ought to be seen as supportive of the Stoic vision of a world in divinely ordered harmony.

See comments relating to 7:1, 32.

Apuleius

Apuleius of Madaurus (c.125 – c.180 CE) was a Platonic philosopher and orator. He trained in Athens and spent time in Rome before returning to Africa. His major work *Metamorphoses* tells the fictional story of Lucius. Lucius is turned into a donkey and has numerous adventures, including his initiation into the mystery cult of Isis at Corinth.

See comments relating to 11:4.

Aristophanes

Aristophanes (c.450 – c.388 BCE) was the greatest of the ancient Greek comedic dramatists. He was both controversial and influential. His relevance to 1 Corinthians is, like Aeschylus, slight and indirect. He makes reference to conventions such as slavery and veil-wearing, which illustrate the history of these topics before the Roman period.

See comments relating to 4:10; 6:20; 11:4.

Aristotle

Aristotle (384 – 322 BCE) belonged to Plato's Academy, before founding his own philosophical school, the Lyceum. He lectured on a wide variety of topics, including logic, nature, theology, ethics, politics, and rhetoric. Many of his ideas were still influential in the first century, although there had been notable development in areas such as rhetoric.

See comments relating to 1:26; 4:10; 9:6; 11:17; 12:12.

Bel and the Dragon

The single chapter that makes up *Bel and the Dragon* is a Greek addition to the book of Daniel, written by 100 BCE. The story adds yet another situation in which Daniel is unfairly conspired against, despite serving God faithfully. As in the other scenarios, Daniel is rescued, his conspirers are punished, and the king turns to honour God. *Bel and the Dragon* serves to mock Gentile idols and illustrate the absurdity of proud defiance of the true God, who saves his faithful people.

See comments relating to 4:9.

Book of the Watchers

This is an apocalyptic work in which the present experience of earthly injustice and subjection to supernatural evil is alleviated by the revelation of God's heavenly justice, which will soon come to earth in the climactic events of divine judgement and deliverance. This work, which forms chapters 1–36 of 1 Enoch, can be dated to some time prior to 160 BCE.

There are elements of such an apocalyptic view that seem to occur in 1 Corinthians, making comparison enlightening.

See comments relating to 2:8; 3:18; 7:26; 11:10; 15:28.

Cicero

Marcus Tullius Cicero (106 – 43 BCE) was a Roman orator who was extremely influential in bringing the ideas of Hellenistic philosophy to Rome, in Latin. Influentially for Roman philosophy, he sought to combine emphases on both philosophy and rhetoric. He had a large literary output, including many letters. These letters provide some insight into conventions of Greco-Roman letter writing.

See comments in relation to 1:1; 2:4; 5:1; 6:4; 9:6.

Demosthenes

Demosthenes (384 – 322 BCE) studied rhetoric under Isaeus and quickly became well known as a speech-writer. He was famously rigorous in training his voice and was greatly honoured as an orator. His speeches opposed Philip and Alexander of Macedon, and after this resistance failed, he ended up taking his own life.

Demosthenes' emphasis on trained oratory is illustrative of an important convention that continued into the Roman period, and was highly esteemed by some in Roman Corinth.

See comments relating to Excursus 5–14; 6:13.

Digesta Iustiniani

The Digesta Iustiniani, or *Pandecta*, is a digest of earlier Roman laws, compiled under Justinian I in the sixth century CE. The relevance here is simply a reference to slavery according to the "law of nations".

See comments relating to 7:21.

Dio Chrysostom

Dio of Prusa, also known as Dio Chrysostom (c.40 – 110 CE), was a Greek orator and philosopher who had been a student of Musonius in the Stoic tradition. After being exiled, he took on the ascetic life of a Cynic, returning after 14 years. He is associated with the beginning of the renewal of Greek rhetoric known as the Second Sophistic.

See comments relating to 1:17, 26; 4:9; 6:4, 12; 7:21; 9:6; 11:33; 12:21; 14:9.

Diodorus Siculus

In his 40–volume *Library* Diodorus Siculus researched and presented the history of the ancient world from mythological beginnings to his own time, the first century BCE. His relevance in this work includes comments about Greek and Roman customs.

See comments relating to 1:10–11, 23; 15:32.

Diogenes Laertius

Diogenes Laertius (early 3rd century) was a biographer of Greek philosophers. His work *Lives of Eminent Philosophers* attempts to summarise the lives and works of numerous important philosophers. The significance for 1 Corinthians is not the reliability of its biographical data, but information about Greco-Roman customs and beliefs.

See comments relating to 4:5, 8, 15.

Epictetus

Epictetus of Hierapolis (c.50 – c.120 CE) was a slave who studied under Musonius and went on to become an important Stoic philosopher as a freedman. He became the head of his own philosophical school in Nicopolis, and his lectures were transcribed by his student Arrian. These lectures especially concern logic and practical ethics. He also argued that the views and practices of the Cynics should be regarded as compatible with Roman Stoicism.

See comments relating to 1:2; 3:1, 10; 4:8, 10; 6:12, 15; 7:9, 21, 32, 38; 9:15, 25; 11:10; 12:15; 15:31.

Epicurus

Epicurus (341 – 270 BCE) was the founder of Epicureanism, which flourished in first century Greek and Roman society. He emphasised the genuineness of empirical knowledge and the freedom of the will. He argued that humans should not be thrown by the unnecessary fear of death, and should rather be free to pursue the enjoyment of appropriate pleasure in this life.

See comments relating to 15:35, 53.

Epistle of Enoch

The *Epistle of Enoch* (1 Enoch 92–105) is based on the idea that righteous Enoch wrote down what was revealed to him before he ascended to heaven. The *Epistle* assures of both blessing and judgement, envisaging the inevitable vindication of the righteous and the certain punishment of their persecutors in a future reversal of fortunes.

See comments relating to Excursus 15; 15:32, 51.

Esther Addition C

In this Greek addition to the earlier form of the book, prayers of Mordecai and Esther are inserted, acknowledging God's role as Israel's saviour.

See comments relating to 3:4.

Euripides

Euripides (c.484 – 406 BCE) is remembered as one of the three great classical Greek tragic dramatists, along with Sophocles and Aeschylus. The play quoted in this book is *The Bacchae*, a work that received first prize in the Athenian drama festival at which it was first performed. It seems that certain religious terminology in this play had lasting influence.[1]

See comments relating to 14:23.

Eusebius of Caesarea

Eusebius (263 – 339 CE) was bishop of Caesarea in the time of Constantine I, and was involved in the Council of Nicea. His most famous work is *Ecclesiastical History*, in which he gives a Christian account of history from the time of the first century. He also wrote other works of history such as the *Life of Constantine* and the work that is cited in this volume, the *Preparation for the Gospel (Praeparatio Evangelica)*. In this work Eusebius makes use of primary sources to relate Christianity to the philosophies and religions that preceded it.

See comments relating to 15:35.

Herodotus

Herodotus of Halicarnassus (c.484 – 430-20 BCE) was a Greek historian from Persian Asia Minor who travelled widely, including to Athens, and went on to write *The Histories*, a foundational landmark in Western historical narrative. His relevance here includes his observation that Greeks of his time thought of themselves as obsessed with wisdom and learning.

See comments relating to 1:22.

Horace

Horace (65 – 8 BCE) was an Augustan poet who studied in Rome and Athens. The philosophy of his poetry and correspondence evidences Epicurean ideals, yet with numerous concessions to other philosophical viewpoints. The relevance to 1 Corinthians in this volume is a passing reference to Jewish sensibilities.

See comments relating to 8:9.

Hymn to Demeter

This Homeric-style song from about the seventh century BCE became the hymn of the Eleusinian mysteries. It relates the foundational myths about Demeter and her daughter Persephone. Persephone is taken down to Hades, and in searching for her, Demeter comes to Eleusis. Eventually an

---

[1] See Thiselton, *First Epistle*, 1126.

arrangement is made whereby Persephone, the goddess of Spring, is able to return to her mother for the majority of each year, bringing fertility with her.

See comments relating to 2:1.

Isocrates

Isocrates (436 – 338 BCE) was a philosopher whom Plato described as a friend of Socrates. He spent several years working as a speech-writer, but was dismissive of the Sophists, whom he claimed cared more for persuasion than truth. He founded a philosophical school in Athens, emphasising the role of rhetoric in engaging in political and ethical discourse.

Isocrates' rejection of the Sophists and advocacy of the appropriate use of rhetoric was greatly influential on classical education. These themes continued to be important in the Roman era.

See comments relating to 1:17; 4:5, 16.

Josephus

Flavius Josephus (37/8 – c.100 CE) was a Jewish priest and military leader. He was involved in the Jewish revolt against the Romans in 66/67 CE. After surrendering to the future emperor Vespasian at Jotapata, he became an advisor to Vespasian's son Titus, who went on to lead the destruction of Jerusalem. Josephus then went to Rome in the service of the Flavian dynasty. His writings about the war and Jewish history evidence both his Jewish background and Roman position.

See comments relating to 1:11, 17, 26; 4:9; Excursus 5–14; 7:10–11, 18; 9:6; 10:11; 11:14, 24; 14:26; Excursus 15; 15:35.

Jubilees

This work arises from the turbulent period of Hellenisation of Antiochus Epiphanes (169 – 164 BCE). It is presented as a secret revelation given to Moses on Mount Sinai and expands on Genesis 1 through to Exodus 12. It advocates the avoidance of Gentile sins and the return to Jewish laws.

See comments relating to Excursus 5–14; 5:5; 11:24.

Judith

This apocryphal book relates the fictional story of the oppression of Nebuchadnezzar on post-exile Israel. Judith leads the nation in begging God to bring about the liberation of his people, and concocts a plan to valiantly bring down the general Holofernes. As in 1 Maccabees, divine intervention is thus conceived of as being anticipated and prompted by active human initiative, even though (at least rhetorically) the free sovereignty of God is staunchly defended. It perhaps dates from the period of the Hasmonean dynasty that followed the Maccabean revolt against Antiochus Epiphanes in the 160s BCE.

See comments relating to Excursus 1–4; 1:26; 2:8, 16; Excursus 15.

Letter of Jeremiah

This literary letter is also known as Baruch 6 and was written some time before 100 BCE. It presents itself as a piece of correspondence from Jeremiah to the Babylonian exiles. Drawing on Jeremiah 10:2–15, the *Letter of Jeremiah* represents an extended diatribe against the idols of the Gentiles: Idols are not real gods, and thus should neither be obeyed nor feared.

See comments relating to 8:4.

Life of Adam and Eve (Greek version)

This work retells the opening events of the book of Genesis. The story deals with the problem of present death, and the promise of future resurrection for those who belong to Adam and Eve's race. The significance of Adam (and death) in the Corinthian correspondence and Romans may indicate that similar motifs were prominent in the first century, but in its present form this work cannot be dated earlier than the second century CE.

See comments relating to 15:10.

Lucretius

Lucretius (c.95 – 54 BCE) was a Roman poet and independent Epicurean philosopher who sought to faithfully present and apply the philosophy of Epicurus himself, for a Roman audience. Like Epicurus, Lucretius urges that fear of death be done away with, in the pursuit of moderate and virtuous happiness.

See comments relating to 15:35.

1 Maccabees

This is a work of historical narrative, showing how the sons of Mattathias resisted the Hellenisation of Antiochus Epiphanes in the 160s BCE. They are depicted as successfully revolting against the Seleucid army, restoring rightful respect for the Torah, and initiating the Hasmonean priestly dynasty. Interestingly, they are presented as being willing to break the Sabbath command in order to attain these goals (2:29–41). Thus, divine intervention is coaxed and fortified by human initiative. This contrasts somewhat with apocalyptic works such as Daniel and 1 Enoch, which rather emphasise the need to wait upon divine timing. The work dates to the early first century BCE.

See comments relating to Excursus 5–14; 7:18.

2 Maccabees

2 Maccabees complements 1 Maccabees by focusing on the role of Judas Maccabeus and providing moving accounts of those who were willing to be martyred rather than accept the dilution of the Torah. It is distanced from the pro-Hasmonean tone of 1 Maccabees, but still offsets the need to wait upon God for vindication with the idea that the right "timing" (8:1–7) justifies a movement from passive (yet noble and self-sacrificial) acceptance of God's discipline to active participation in God's work of violent vindication. It probably dates to the early first century BCE.

See comments relating to 1:3; 2:8; Excursus 5–14; 11:32; 15:24, 45.

3 Maccabees

Like the Biblical books of Daniel and Esther, 3 Maccabees explores divine judgement on boastful rulers and divine vindication of God's faithful people. The situation is different to that of 1 and 2 Maccabees: The boastful ruler is Ptolemy IV (third century BCE); and his oppressive acts include attempting to enter the holy of holies in Jerusalem, attempting to enslave the Alexandrian Jews, and attempting to kill all the Jews of Egypt. But God acts to save and vindicate his persecuted people. The work can perhaps be dated to the first century BCE.

See comments relating to 12:2; Excursus 15.

4 Maccabees

This work is introduced as a philosophical treatise. The thesis of this treatise is that "godly reason is master of the passions"; that is, that life under the Torah successfully curbs irrational passions. The case study is the situation of Eleazar, the mother, and the seven brothers of 2 Maccabees 6–7. Because of the rational wisdom that comes from the law, these figures are willing to be martyred by a tyrant rather than pursue the pleasures associated with the full acceptance of Hellenisation. It may date to the early first century CE.

See comments relating to 2:14; 4:16; Excursus 5–14; 8:4; 13:13.

Maximus of Tyre

Maximus of Tyre (second century CE) was a travelling Greek orator and philosopher. His forty-one extant discourses cover a variety of themes from a broadly Platonic perspective. His relevance to 1 Corinthians is his utilisation of a conventional metaphor of the body.

See comments relating to 12:12.

Musonius Rufus

Gaius Musonius Rufus (c.30 – 101 CE) was an important Roman Stoic philosopher who lectured in Greek. Twenty-one of his discourses were recorded by his student Lucius. These especially emphasise the ways in which philosophy ought to result in a moral life.

See comments relating to 6:7; 7:1; 11:14.

Ocellus Lucanas

Ocellus Lucanas was a Pythagorean philosopher from the fifth century BCE. His relevance to this volume is simply that a Stoic work from the mid-second century BCE is mistakenly attributed to him, and continues to bear his name. The work is *On the Nature of the Universe*.[2] In terms of its relevance to this book, the work exhibits a Stoic vision of marriage in which one finds harmony with the will of God by pursuing marital procreation.

See comments relating to 7:1.

Pausanius

Pausanius the Geographer (prior to 176 CE) travelled throughout Asia Minor, Italy and Greece. His lengthy *Description of Greece* depicts the natural and human-made sights of his travels, as well as their historical and religious significance. There are numerous enlightening comments about Roman Corinth, albeit from a century after the time of 1 Corinthians.

See comments relating to 1:14, 26; 2:1; 10:25; 15:6.

---

[2] See the discussion in Will Deming, *Paul on Marriage & Celibacy: The Hellenistic Background of 1 Corinthians 7*, 2nd Edition (Grand Rapids, Michigan, Eerdmans, 2004).

Philo of Alexandria

Philo (c.15 BCE – c.50 CE) came from a wealthy Alexandrian family and wrote extensively about the Pentateuch. He insisted on both literal and allegorical readings of Scripture, using his Hellenistic education to defend and explain the Torah. Philo is thought of as a Jewish philosopher, engaging overtly with Greek philosophy in his biblical expositions, and bringing to them the worldviews of Platonism and Stoicism.

See comments relating to 1:17, 26; 3:1, 3–4, 10; 4:10, 15; Excursus 5–14; 5:1, 7, 9–10; 6:13; 7:18, 22, 32; 8:6; 9:9, 22; 10:4; 11:5, 21; 12:21; 13:1, 11, 12; 14:11, 15, 32; Excursus 15; 15:8, 19, 24, 32, 45, 49, 52–53.

Plato

Plato (c.429 – 347 BCE), a student of Socrates, founded the Academy. All of his works survive and almost all are in the form of dialogues. In most of these the primary speaker is Plato's mentor, Socrates. The ways in which these dialogues represent Plato's own philosophy are debated, but the topics they raise have been extremely influential. These include the place of rhetoric, the question of perception and reality, the nature of the human, and the ideal state.

Plato's ideas remained influential in the first century, and even if they were not consciously discussed by the Christians to whom Paul wrote, form one important cultural background.

See comments relating to 1:17; Excursus 5–14; 6:13; 9:3, 25; 12:26; 13:1; 15:32, 35.

Pliny the Younger

Pliny the Younger (61/2 – c.113 CE) was a Roman lawyer, author, and letter-writer who held a series of significant positions in Rome. He published books of his letters covering a range of topics, including correspondence with the Emperor Trajan. In this volume his comments about a Roman meal provide some illumination of what might have been happening in Roman Corinth.

See comments relating to 11:21.

Plutarch

Plutarch (c.45 – c.120) was a Greek biographer and lay Platonist philosopher who became a Roman citizen. He was critical of both the Epicureans and the Stoics, while approving of certain Stoic values. His

Lives provides biographies of a great number of significant Greco-Roman figures.

See comments relating to 1:11, 17, 31; 4:8; 6:5; 7:1; 9:25; 11:4; 14:2, 35; 15:6, 35, 53.

Polybius

Polybius (c.200 – 120 BCE) was one of a number of Greek intellectuals whose involvement in Rome in the mid-second century BCE marked a turning point in the receptivity of Rome to Greek intellectual ideas. His relevance in this volume is his description of certain historical events in his *Histories*.

See comments relating to 1:11.

Prayer of Azariah and the Song of the Three Young Men

This addition to the biblical book of Daniel supplements the narrative of Daniel 3 with a prayer of national confession by Azariah (Abednego) and a song of praise from Daniel's three friends. This latter portion rehearses the events of God's miraculous rescue from the fire, and depicts a response of psalm-like thanksgiving.

See comments relating to 15:57.

Pseudo-Eupolemus

Pseudo-Eupolemus is the anonymous author of two fragments that have been preserved in quotations in Eusebius of Caesarea's *Preparation for the Gospel*. The author is believed to be Samaritan, and relates stories known from Genesis in a way that makes use of Greek tradition. The excerpts probably date from some time prior to 160 BCE.

See comments relating to Excursus 5–14.

Pseudo-Phocylides

The *Sentences* of Pseudo-Phocylides are a Jewish poetic piece of 230 lines. The work is difficult to date, but shows a certain affinity with the thought of Stoic writers of the first century such as Musonius Rufus; and evidences openness toward Hellenistic culture. It may be, then, that it dates from the period between 30 BCE and 40 CE.[3] The work presents many

[3] See P.W. Van Der Horst, *The Sentences of Pseudo-Phocylides with Introduction and Commentary* (Leiden, Brill, 1978), 82.

themes of the Torah in a way that addresses a Hellenised Jewish audience.

See comments relating to 1:11, 31; Excursus 5–14; 5:1; 7:14, 36–8; 9:19–22; 11:4, 14; 15:35.

Psalms of Solomon

These Psalms were probably originally composed in Hebrew and express responses to the events associated with the Roman incursion into Jerusalem under Pompey in 63 BCE, and possibly the siege of Jerusalem under Herod the Great in 37 BCE. The Psalms may represent a Pharisaic perspective, seeking to point to acts of individual immorality and corporate impurity as the reason for God's allowance of the Roman invasions. The edited collection of Psalms probably dates from the end of the first century BCE.[4]

See comments relating to Excursus 5–14, 5:1, 7; 15:35.

Quintilian

Marcus Fabius Quintilianus (35 – post-96 CE) was a Roman orator who taught rhetoric in Rome. His work on theoretical and practical rhetoric, *Institutes of Oratory*, is considered to be a major contribution to literary criticism. This work presents oratory according to five rules: *Inventio* (invention); *dispositio* (arrangement); *elocutio* (style); *memoria* (memorisation); and *pronuntiatio* (delivery).

See comments relating to 2:4; 4:16; 7:1; 10:11.

Qumran Literature (Focus: Thanksgiving Psalms 1QH)

The Qumran community was a sectarian group based near the Dead Sea. 1QH[a] was among the first of the Dead Sea Scrolls to be discovered. This *Hodayot* (Thanksgivings) Scroll contains a number of non-canonical psalm-like compositions in Hebrew. They probably date to the end of the second century BCE; but their authorship (perhaps the Teacher of Righteousness) and intended use (whether for corporate covenant renewal or private devotion) are debated. The *Hodayot* evidence the sectarian and apocalyptic viewpoints of the Qumran community.

For all references to Qumran literature, see comments relating to 3:9, 16; 6:3; 11:10; 14:26; Excursus 15.

---

[4] See Robert B. Wright, *The Psalms of Solomon, A Critical Edition of the Greek Text* (London: T&T Clark, 2007), 6–7.

Rhetorica Ad Herennium

The *Rhetorica Ad Herennium* is a work from the early first century BCE, which was formerly thought to be by Cicero. It is a Latin book about rhetoric and has enjoyed ongoing influence.

See comments relating to 2:1.

Seneca

Lucius Annaeus Seneca (c.4 BCE – 65 CE) was a Roman Stoic philosopher, orator, dramatist, letter-writer and statesman. He studied rhetoric in Rome before falling out with the emperor Caligula. He was exiled by the subsequent emperor, Claudius, but later recalled as a tutor for the young Nero. He went on to advise Nero as emperor, but was eventually implicated in an assassination plot and ordered by Nero to commit suicide. Like the earlier Cicero, one of his contributions was to bring Greek philosophy into Roman (Latin) discussion.

See comments relating to 2:13; 3:5; 4:10; 6:13, 15; 7:21; 8:6; 9:25.

Sextus Empiricus

Sextus Empiricus (late 2nd century CE) was a Sceptic philosopher and physician. He was highly critical of Stoicism, and so his work provides a useful view of the reception of Stoic logic from an unsympathetic perspective.

See comments relating to 15:35.

Sibylline Oracles

The Sibylline Oracles are a collection of Jewish works written in the style of a "Sibyl" or seer, who is unwillingly seized by God for prophetic utterances. Book 3 appears to be the earliest of these works, perhaps written in the Roman province of Asia between 80 and 40 BCE.[5] The Sibyl is presented as being the daughter or niece of Noah, prophesying about future events from that earlier time (3.813–829).

See comments relating to Excursus 5–14; 11:4.

---

[5] See Rieuwerd Buitenwerf, *Book III of the Sibylline Oracles and Its Social Setting* (Leiden, Brill, 2003), for a defence of this provenance and dating.

Sirach

The Wisdom of Ben Sira, also known as *Sirach or Ecclesiasticus*, is an apocryphal wisdom book dating from the early second century BCE, translated into its Greek form at the end of that century. It consists of the collected works of Joshua Ben Sira, utilising a number of different genres, but predominantly proverbs. A key theme is the identification of wisdom with the Torah.

See comments relating to 1:31; 3:4; Excursus 5–14; 6:3, 16; 7:9, 36; 15:36, 55.

Sophocles

Along with Aeschylus and Euripides, Sophocles (c.496 – 406 BCE) was one of the great early Greek tragic dramatists. He received popular and critical acclaim during his lifetime and has had enduring influence. In the present work, however, his relevance is minimal. He simply provides examples of conventional Greco-Roman *topoi*.

See comments relating to 1:11; 14:2.

Stobaeus

John Stobaeus (5th century CE) was a compiler of materials from Greek authors. The relevance in this volume is his summary of the Stoic Zeno's interest in the stars.

See comments relating to 15:40.

Strabo

Strabo (64/3 BCE – 23 CE) was a Greek geographer and historian. Together with the later Pausanius, his comments about Roman Corinth provide important insight into the ancient city's landmarks.

See comments relating to 1:26; 2:1; 9:24; 15:32.

Suetonius

Gaius Suetonius Tranquillis (69 – post-122 CE) was a Roman historian and biographer. He was a friend of Pliny the Younger and wrote about Greek and Roman lives and pastimes. His popular work about the first eleven Roman emperors, *Lives of the Caesars*, captured the imagination of the public with anecdotal evidence of the rulers' often-scandalous lives.

See comments relating to 1:23; 7:26.

Testament of Abraham

This Christian work tells the story of Abraham's death. God sends Michael to tell Abraham that the time has come for his death. Abraham refuses the command to give his final testament, so God orders Death to come in disguise. After learning that God shows compassion to sinners, Abraham is taken by God – without ever giving his testament. It may date to the first or second century CE, and probably updates a previously existing Jewish work.

See comments relating to 3:13; 6:3; 15:55.

Testament of Job

This is a Jewish retelling of the story of Job in the form of a final testament from Job's perspective. Job is presented as a heroic king who is converted from idolatry and challenges Satan head-on. The work thus explores the relationship between the two settings of heaven and earth. It probably dates to the second century CE.

See comments relating to 14:4.

Testaments of the Twelve Patriarchs

The *Testaments of the Twelve Patriarchs* presents final "testaments" from the lips of each of the tribal founders of Israel, warning their descendants to learn from their own experiences. Throughout the *Testaments* Joseph is presented as a model of piety, while Judah and Levi are honoured as representing royalty and priesthood respectively. In their present form the *Testaments* are probably an early Christian edition of an earlier Jewish product, evidencing continuity with Jewish ethical topics and argumentation.[6]

See comments relating to Excursus 5–14; 5:7, 10–11; 6:18; 7:1; Excursus 15.

Theognis

Theognis of Megara was a Greek elegiac poet from the 6th century BCE. His relevance here is his adoption of the motif of the "rock-clinging polyp", which changes according to its environment.

See comments relating to 9:19–22.

---

[6] Martinus De Jonge, *Pseudepigrapha of the Old Testament as Part of Christian Literature: The Case of the Testaments of the Twelve Patriarchs and the Greek Life of Adam and Eve* (Leiden, Brill, 2003), 177.

Tobit

The book of Tobit is an apocryphal wisdom tale with certain broad similarities to the biblical book of Job. It relates the story of Tobit, a righteous Israelite who has been exiled under King Shalmaneser of Assyria. Despite faithfully giving alms and burying the dead, he suffers unwarranted affliction. He is ultimately restored by God, and praises the "King of Heaven" who restores the righteous. The book may date to the reign of Antiochus Ephiphanes (175 – 164 BCE), when burying the dead was forbidden for faithful Jews.

See comments relating to 7:1.

Watchers, Book of the

See *Book of the Watchers* above.

Wisdom of Solomon

This apocryphal wisdom book, written from the perspective of Solomon, contains the "book of eschatology" (1:1–6:11) in which the fates of the righteous and their persecutors are considered; the "book of wisdom" (6:12–9:18) in which Wisdom is personified; and the "book of history" (10–19) in which God's judgement of the nations is explored. It may date to the first century BCE or early first century CE.

See comments relating to Excursus 1–4; 1:30; 2:6, 16; 3:13; 4:1; Excursus 5–14; 6:3; 8:4; 10:1, 4; 11:32; 14:23; Excursus 15; 15:19, 21, 35, 53.

The World of 1 Corinthians:

1 Corinthians and Illuminating Backgrounds

Greetings and Thanksgiving

1:1–9: Greetings and Thanksgiving

1:1 Paul, called to be an apostle of Christ Jesus, through the will of God; and
Sosthenes the brother, 2 to the church of God that is in Corinth, sanctified in
Christ Jesus, called to be holy, together with all those who call upon the name
of our Lord Jesus Christ in every place – both their Lord and ours. 3 Grace to
you and peace from God our father and our Lord Jesus Christ.

Paul… and Sosthenes
Most letters of this time and place name only one sender. Cicero appears to mention close family members as co-senders in *Letter to Atticus*, 11.5.1 and a few other letters, and there are other examples in papyri, but the practice is not the norm. It would seem reasonable to infer that "and Sosthenes" here indicates that Sosthenes had a role in the creation of the letter – a role not shared by those who simply add "greetings" at the ending of the letter.[1]

Acts 18 reports that a synagogue ruler in Corinth was named Sosthenes. If this is Paul's co-sender, it may be speculated that his familiarity with the Jewish Scriptures and worship had some influence in the formation of the letter.

All those who call upon the name of our Lord Jesus Christ
The motif of "calling upon the name of the Lord" is often used in the Old Testament (e.g. Genesis 4:26; 1 Kings 18:24; 1 Chronicles 16:8; Psalm 116:13,17; Isaiah 64:7; Lamentations 3:55; Joel 2:32; Zephaniah 3:9; Zechariah 13:9) in relation to "the Lord" God.

"Calling upon" ("invoking") a god was a common theme of Greco-Roman religion:

---

[1] See E. Randolph Richards, *Paul and First-Century Letter Writing: Secretaries, Composition and Collection* (Downers Grove, Illinois, InterVarsity Press, 2004). From 645 ancient letters, Richards finds six examples that include co-senders in an equivalent way.

Epictetus: Discourses, 2.7.12–13[2]
Calling upon the god, we plead to the interpreter, "Lord, have mercy! Permit me to come out of this!"

Grace to you
Paul's greeting, "Grace" (χάρις) is a Christianised version of the conventional epistolary expression "Greetings" (χαίρειν):

2 Maccabees 1:10[3]
Greetings [χαίρειν] and good health!

Oxyrhynchus papyrus 292 (25 CE)
Theon, to the honourable Tyrannus: Many greetings!

To the church of God that is in Corinth

The site of Ancient Corinth

1:4 I thank my God always concerning you, because of the grace of God, which
he has given you in Christ Jesus – 5 because in every way you have been made
rich in him, in all speech and all knowledge, 6 just as the testimony of Christ
has been confirmed among you, 7 so that you are not lacking in any gift as you
eagerly await the revelation of our Lord Jesus Christ, 8 who will also keep you
firm until the end, blameless on the day of our Lord Jesus. 9 God is faithful,
through whom you were called into fellowship with his son, Jesus Christ our
Lord.

2 This comes in the context of a discussion on "how we ought to use divination".

3 This is the beginning of a letter form.

I thank my God always concerning you
A thanksgiving or prayer is a conventional part of the opening of a Greco-Roman letter, as can be seen in the other letters of the New Testament, and the example below:[4]

> *Papyrus letter from Serenos to Isadora: Oxyrhynchus papyrus 528 (Second century* CE*)*
> Serenos, to Isadora, sister and lady: Heartiest greetings. Before everything else, I pray for your health; and each day and evening I bow down for you before Theoris who loves you. I want you to know…

The day of our Lord Jesus
This phrase "the day of the Lord" is used in prophetic literature of the Old Testament in reference to "the LORD" God (e.g. Isaiah 13:6; Ezekiel 13:5; Joel 1:15).

[4] For discussions and examples of early letter writing see: Abraham J. Malherbe, *Ancient Epistolary Theorists* (The Society of Biblical Literature, 1988); Jerome Murphy-O'Connor, *Paul the Letter-Writer: His World, His Options, His Skills* (Collegeville, Minnesota, The Liturgical Press, 1995); Stanley K. Stowers, *Letter Writing in Greco-Roman Antiquity* (Philadelphia, The Westminster Press, 1986); Hans-Josef Klauck, *Ancient Letters and the New Testament: A Guide to Context and Exegesis* (Waco, Texas, Baylor University Press, 2006); and Hermann Probst, *Paulus und der Brief: Die Rhetorik des antiken Briefes als Form der paulinischen Korintherkorrespondenz (1 Kor 8–10)*, (Tübingen, Mohr Siebeck, 1991).

The Cross Confronts Divisive Autonomous Boasting in Human Wisdom

Excursus: Chapters 1–4 and Reversal

One important theme evident in these chapters (along with chapter 15) is the dual motif of the *condemned boaster* and the *vindicated sufferer*. This motif is well attested in the Old Testament and Jewish literature, and essential for early Christian reception of Jesus. Paul seems to be interpreting the Corinthians as behaving like the boastful human rulers of this age (who will be condemned) rather than the humble cruciform apostles (who await resurrected vindication in Christ).

According to this flexible early Jewish motif, there are the *rulers* (ἀρχή/ἄρχων/βασιλεύω etc.), who are emphatically *human* (ἄνθρωπος), and who defiantly boast (καυχάομαι) and think themselves to be *wise* (σοφός), but who will be *destroyed* (φθείρω etc.). On the other side there are the *righteous* (δίκαιος) who are the genuine recipients of revealed *wisdom* (σοφία) from God in the form of a *mystery* (μυστήριον), and who come close to (or experience) *death* (θάνατος/νεκρός/ἀποθνῄσκω), but can expect divinely granted *victory* (νῖκος), perhaps in the form of *resurrection* (ἐγείρομαι/ἀνάστασις).

In addition to the illustrative texts given in context below, note the following:

Psalm 2:2 (Septuagint)
The kings of the earth have risen up, and the rulers have gathered together against the Lord, and against his anointed [Christ].

Psalm 9:20–21 (Septuagint)
Let the nations know that they are *human*.

Daniel 2:19–23 (Septuagint)
[After the king's wise men fail and all are threatened with death:]
Then the mystery was revealed to Daniel in a vision of the night, and he blessed the God of heaven. And Daniel said, "May the name of God be blessed from eternity to eternity, because wisdom [σοφία] and understanding [σύνεσις] are his! He changes seasons and times. He appoints and deposes kings. He gives wisdom to the wise and understanding to those with understanding. He reveals the deep and hidden things, knowing the things in darkness, and light is with him. To you, O God of my fathers, I will give blessing and praise, because you have given me wisdom and power, and have now made known to me that which we asked of you – you have made known the vision of the king."

Judith 9:7–9[1]
For see: The Assyrians have increased in their power, exalting themselves because of horse and rider, priding themselves in the strength of their army, placing their hope in shield and spear and bow and sling; and they do not know that you are the Lord who crushes wars. The Lord is your name. You throw down the strong in your power, and you bring down their might in your wrath. For they have conspired to pollute your holy places, to defile the resting place of your glorious name, to cut down the horns of your altar with iron. Look at their arrogance, and send your wrath upon their heads.

Wisdom of Solomon 6:1–5[2]
Listen then, kings, and understand! Learn, judges of the ends of the earth! Give ear, you who rule over many and boast over the multitudes of the nations: Your rule was given to you by the Lord, and your power from the Most High. He will examine your works and will search out your plans, because as assistants of his kingdom you did not judge rightly or keep his law, or go along with his purposes. Shockingly and hastily, he will come upon you, because severe judgement comes to those in positions of authority.

Paul summons the Corinthians to abandon their envy of the "rulers of this age", and to imitate his own inhabitation of the cross, thereby boasting "in God" rather than "in humans". It is not until chapter 15, however, that Paul emphasises that those who inhabit death in this way are heading for the vindication of resurrection.

---

1 This is part of Judith's prayer on behalf of persecuted Israel, reminding God that he is the one who brings down the boastful but lifts up the oppressed.

2 This comes after an extended promise that God will zealously repel all of his enemies in vindicating his righteous people.

1:10–2:5: God's Cross and Human Wisdom

1:10 I appeal to you, brothers and sisters, through the name of our Lord Jesus Christ, that you all speak the same, and that there be no divisions among you; but that you be restored in the same mind and in the same purpose. 11 For it has been revealed to me by Chloe's people, my brothers and sisters, that there is strife among you.

There is strife among you

Depictions of political "division" by Greco-Roman speakers and writers often include the problems of "zeal" and "strife", and call for unity of mind and purpose:

> *Diodorus Siculus: Library, 12.66.2*[3]
> When the treason became obvious to all throughout the city, and the multitudes were divided into factions – those wishing to fight with the Athenians, and those wishing to help the Lakedemonians – a certain person, acting on his own initiative, proclaimed that those who wished could take up arms with the Athenians and Megarians.

> *Sophocles: Oedipus at Colonus, 1230–1235*[4]
> As when he has reached the end of youth, bearing its light follies, what plagues are outside a person's great suffering? Are there any troubles a person doesn't experience? Envy, factions, strife, fights, and murders.

> *Polybius: The Histories, 5.104.1*[5]
> He said that the most important thing is that Greeks should never go to war against one another, but should have great thankfulness to the gods, if, all speaking as one, and combining their hands together as those crossing a river, they are together able to save themselves and their cities from slaughter, repelling the inroads of the Barbarians.

---

[3] Diodorus' account of battle and betrayal is simply notable for using the same terms that Paul uses in 1 Corinthians to depict division and factions.

[4] This is a description of the social experience of middle age. Here it is simply illustrative of the fact that influential Greek literature commonly combined the problems of zeal and strife, as Paul goes on to do in 1 Corinthians.

[5] The context is the description of a powerful speech that brought success through the pursuit of harmony. For a similar example, see Aristotle, *Politics*, 2.3.3.

> *Plutarch: Lives, Caesar, 32.2–3*[6]
> For conflicting passions and violent motions prevailed in every place. For those rejoicing did not keep quiet but came face to face with those who were in much fear and suffering in such a great city; and, being arrogant about what was coming, came into strife with them.

Jewish writers, similarly, appeal for harmony in the face of divisive "strife":

> *Pseudo-Phocylides: Sentences, 74–75*[7]
> They [that is, the sun and the moon] always have harmony; for if there were strife among the blessed ones, heaven would not stand.

> *Josephus: Jewish War, 5.3956*[8]
> When did our bondage begin? Was it not from the factions of our forefathers, when the madness of Aristobulus and Hyrcanus, and our quarrels between one another brought Pompey to the city, and God subjected to the Romans those not worthy of freedom?

> *Josephus: AJ, 12.283*[9]
> But especially I urge you to be like-minded; and in whatever way one of you surpasses another, defer to one another, making the best use of your virtues.

1:12 Now what I am saying is this: That each of you says, "I belong to Paul", or
"I belong to Apollos" or "I belong to Cephas" or "I belong to Christ". 13 Has
Christ been divided? Paul was not crucified for you, was he? Or were you bap-
tised into the name of Paul? 14 I am thankful that I baptised none of you except
for Crispus and Gaius, 15 so that none of you might say that you were baptised
into my name! 16 I did also baptise the household of Stephanas. Besides that I
do not know if I baptised anyone else.

"I belong to Paul"
This language of "belonging" may be Paul's pejorative way of encapsulating Corinthian divisions that he perceives as childish.[10]

---

6 This is part of a section describing internal agitations in Rome.

7 This occurs within a section that cautions against envy.

8 The mention of "quarrels" here illustrates the use of the same term that Paul uses (translated as "strife") to depict relational bickering.

9 Josephus is quoting Mattathias' instructions to his sons.

10 Margaret M. Mitchell argues that a significant background is the language of parent-child and master-slave relationships: Margaret M. Mitchell, *Paul and the Rhetoric of Reconciliation* (Louisville, Kentucky, Westminster John Knox Press, 1991), 85.

It seems that believers in Corinth were disputing the authority of local leaders (such as Stephanas: 16:15), and debating the relative merits of external leaders.[11]

I baptised . . .

It appears that the boastful divisions in Corinth related in some way to baptism at Corinth. Strabo and Pausanius report that Roman Corinth was well supplied with fresh water, and had many fountains.

Fountains in Roman Corinth, such as the fountains of Glauke (left; located near the temple of Octavia) and Peirene (right), were generally dedicated to deities.

Baptisms may well have taken place at one of the two seas between which Corinth was positioned. Opposite are views of the Gulf of Corinth, to the north of the ancient city:

[11] For an exploration of leadership in Corinth see Andrew D. Clarke, *Secular and Christian Leadership in Corinth: A Socio-Historical and Exegetical Study of 1 Corinthians 1–6* (Milton Keynes, Paternoster, 2006).

Pausanius: Description of Greece, 2.1.2
Now the Isthmus of the Corinthians stretches out on the one side toward Cenchreae, and on the other toward the Lechaion Sea.

Baptism in Corinth is mentioned in Acts 18:8. Apollos is introduced later in the same chapter (24–27).

1:17 **For Christ did not send me to baptise, but to proclaim the gospel, not in the wisdom of speech [ἐν σοφίᾳ λόγου], in order that the cross of Christ might not be made empty.**

To proclaim the gospel
In Paul's slightly later letter to the Romans, he depicts himself as assuming the role of the Isaianic servant, in bringing the gospel to the nations (Romans 15:17–21, quoting Isaiah 52:15). It may be that this self-understanding – as the servant of the Servant – had been fundamental for Paul since his Damascus Road experience, lying behind his frequent self-designations as a servant (e.g. 3:5). Just as the Isaianic Servant is sent to bring light to the nations, so Paul has been sent to proclaim the gospel.

The plural noun "gospel" was sometimes used in Roman imperial propaganda, such as the reference to the impact of Augustus on the world in the Priene Calendar Inscription:[12]

---

12 As well as the Priene Inscription, see the political use of this term in Josephus, *Jewish War*, 4.10.6; 4.11.5. For a succinct summary of imperial presence in Corinth, see Ben Witherington III, *Conflict and Community in Corinth: A Socio-Rhetorical Commentary on 1 and 2 Corinthians* (Carlisle, Paternoster; Grand Rapids, Michigan, Eerdmans; 1995), 295–298.

Inscription: Priene (9 BCE)

This seemed fitting to the Greeks of Asia, in the opinion of the high priest Apollonius of Menophilos Azantius: "Seeing as everything in our life has been arranged by the effort of Providence, and our life has been granted the greatest honour in the coming of Augustus, who for the benefaction of humans was filled by Providence with virtue. He was sent to be a saviour for ourselves and those after us. He is the one who will put an end to war, and set everything in place. And in his coming, Caesar has surpassed the expectations of all of the preceding *gospels*, not only surpassing the preceding benefactors, but not even giving any hope that those who follow him might surpass him. And this god's birthday inaugurated the *gospels* [i.e. the great news], which came about because of him, for the sake of the world." This is what the people of Asia resolved in Smyrna.

Not in the wisdom of speech

"Wisdom" was valued in the Greco-Roman world, as seen most obviously in the philosophical schools of the era. In mid-first century Corinth, Roman values were especially celebrated, which probably means that the schools of Stoicism and Epicureanism (which were fashionable in Rome) were held in high esteem. Plato's legacy, likewise, had not disappeared. Josephus acknowledges the wisdom of the philosophers, but claims that they had attained it by following Moses.

Plato: Apology of Socrates, 23a–b[13]

On each of these occasions, those who are present think me to be wise when I reprove another. But dare I say it, O people, it is God who is wise, and in this oracle says this: "Human wisdom is of little worth, and is nothing". And it appears to say this of "Socrates" merely to use my name, making me an example, so as to say, "This one of you, O humans, is wise: The one who knows, as Socrates, that you are nothing with respect to true wisdom".

Josephus: Against Apion, 2.281 [Cf. 223–4, where Plato is named as relatively admirable][14]

For first of these [Gentile imitators of Judaism] were the Greek philosophers, for whom it seemed that they observed their forefathers; but who in

[13] Although this passage bears some similarities to Paul's argument, it is important to recall that Paul is not simply being self-effacing. For Paul, divine wisdom is inaccessible apart from the "mystery" of Jesus Christ, revealed by his Spirit.

[14] Josephus is arguing that the persistence of Judaism over time is evidence of its worthiness.

deeds and in philosophy followed that one [i.e. Moses], similarly thinking about God, and teaching simplicity of life and fellowship with one another.

However, although Plato valued "wisdom", he was suspicious of "speech" or "rhetoric", as practised by the Sophists.[15] The Sophists aimed to make an art of persuasion, but were arguably uninterested in whether or not their persuasions aligned with "truth" (cf. Aristotle, *Rhetoric*, 1.1–3, 1.1.11).

Isocrates: Against the Sophists, 13.10[16]
But they [those who teach political discourse in the manner of the Sophists] say that the knowledge of matters can be passed on just as easily as the knowledge of the alphabet, as if one can have both of these without having made a proper examination. They imagine that because of the extravagance of their promises they will command awe, and the instruction of their speeches will seem to be of great worth. They fail to realise that it is not those who dare to *boast* about the arts who make them great, but those who have the power to search out all that may be found in them.

Philo: Every Good Man is Free, 4
Now I am speaking of those who are unclean, meaning those who have never tasted education, or those who act treacherously: Having received education in a crooked way, they have transformed the beauty of wisdom [σοφίας] into the ugliness of sophistry [σοφιστείας].

Dio Chrysostom describes a trip to Corinth, perhaps late in the first century, at which time the "disciples" of the Sophists clamoured for esteem. The scene is reminiscent of the divisions that Paul recounts: "I belong to Paul . . . I belong to Apollos . . ."

Dio Chrysostom: Eighth Discourse: On Virtue (Diogenes), 8.4b–6[17]
When Antisthenes died, and, of the others, he [Diogenes, but arguably a covert reference to Dio himself] considered none worthy of association, he

[15] Of the many discussions of 1 Corinthians in relation to Greco-Roman rhetoric and Sophistry, see Duane Litfin, *St. Paul's Theology of Proclamation: 1 Corinthians 1–4 and Greco-Roman Rhetoric* (Cambridge, Cambridge University Press, 1994); Bruce W. Winter, *Philo and Paul Among the Sophists: Alexandrian and Corinthian Responses to a Julio-Claudian Movement*, 2nd Ed. (Grand Rapids, Michigan/ Cambridge, U.K., Eerdmans, 2002); and Stephen M. Pogoloff, *Logos and Sophia: The Rhetorical Situation of 1 Corinthians* (Atlanta Georgia, Scholars Press, 1992).

[16] Isocrates is developing his assertion that they have no concern for the *truth*.

[17] This describes a trip of Diogenes to Corinth, but arguably represents the story of Dio's own trip to Corinth in the late first century.

departed to Corinth. And there he dwelt, neither renting a house nor staying with someone else, but camping in Craneion. For he observed that many people gathered there on account of the harbours and the *hetairas*, and because the city was situated as if it were in the middle of Greece. Therefore, just as it is prudent for a man, as a good doctor, to offer his services where there are many who are sick, so, where there are many who are foolish, the wise man should go, reproving and convicting their folly. So when it came time for the Isthmian games, and all were in Isthmia, he too went down there.

8.8
But when he said that all following his direction would be relieved of folly and wickedness and lack of self-control, no one came to him or sought to be cured by him . . . [evidently not concerned about a] soul that was foolish and untaught and cowardly and rash and pleasure-loving and illiberal and wrathful and unkind and wicked and in every way corrupted.

8.9
And there at this time, around the temple of Poseidon, one could hear many of the wicked Sophists, crying out and reviling one another, and their so-called disciples fighting one another . . . [and] myriads of lawyers, twisting judgements.

8.36
Immediately then the masses scorned him and said he was mad; and again the Sophists raised a noise, just as frogs in a pond who don't see the water-snake.

Plutarch describes the attitude of the famous Greek orator Demosthenes:

Plutarch: Lives, Demosthenes, 7.2[18]
And being persuaded of how much acting adds adornment and grace to speech [λόγῳ], he considered the practice of declamation without consideration of delivery and disposition to be worth little – or even nothing.

The dedication of a statue to a well-known orator in the *agora* of Ancient Corinth indicates the esteem that was attached to worthy orators by the time of Marcus Aurelius. Although the orator was based elsewhere, Corinth boasted a connection as the "mother city":

---

[18] As Plutarch hints, Demosthenes was famous for the lengths to which he went in order to perfect his voice and performance.

Inscription: Statue base from agora (time of Marcus Aurelius)
Peducaeus Cestianus, the Apollonian orator. By decree of Corinth, the mother-city.

1:18 For the message of the cross, to those who are being destroyed, is foolishness; but to those who are being saved – to us – it is the power of God. 19 For it is written:

I will destroy the wisdom of the wise, and I will reject the understanding of those with understanding.

20 Where is the wise person? Where is the scribe? Where is the debater of this age? Has God not made foolish the world's wisdom?

I will destroy the wisdom of the wise
The "wisdom of humans" features as a theme in Isaiah, where it is depicted as bold defiance against God, who is to be trusted in spite of the apparent strength of adversaries (19:11–12; 44:25). The quote is from Isaiah 29:14, and reproduces the Septuagint exactly, except for the word "reject" (ἀθετήσω). The Septuagint has "conceal" (κρύψω), but such a word would be confusing in the context of 1 Corinthians, where Paul insists that *God's wisdom* is hidden.

The antithesis between "being destroyed" (or "perishing") and "being saved" exemplifies the motif of dual reversal that is explored in the excursus on chapters 1–4.

1:21 For seeing as, in God's wisdom, the world did not know God through its wisdom, God was pleased to save those who believe through the foolishness of proclamation. 22 For Jews ask for signs and Gentiles seek wisdom; 23 but we proclaim a crucified Christ, a cause of offence to Jews and foolishness to Gentiles. 24 But to those who are called, both Jews and Gentiles, Christ is the power of God and the wisdom of God. 25 For the foolishness of God is wiser than humans, and the weakness of God is stronger than humans.

Jews ask for signs and Gentiles seek wisdom
Each of the four canonical Gospels presents a Jewish suspicion of Jesus that is expressed in asking for miraculous evidence of his implied Messianic claims. See, for example, Matthew 12:38–9; 16:1–4; and 24:3.

Acts 17:21 remarks that the Athenians spent their time doing nothing but discussing the latest ideas. Herodotus reports a similar characterisation of the Greeks:

Herodotus: Histories, 4.77.1–2[19]
And indeed, I have also heard something else, told by the Peloponnesians. Anacharsis had been sent by the king of the Scythians, to become a student of the ways of the Greek. Following his return home, he said to the one who had sent him, "All of the Greeks are untiring in their pursuit of all kinds of wisdom – except for the Lakedemonians; but it is these alone who sensibly both give and receive reason." But this is a story pointlessly put together by the Greeks themselves; and the man in question, as earlier mentioned, was put to death.

A crucified Christ, a cause of stumbling . . . and foolishness
Crucifixion was considered a particularly cruel form of execution. Diodorus Siculus mentions crucifixion as an example of the Carthaginians' savagery:

Diodorus Siculus: Library, 13.111.4[20]
For the misfortune that had happened to Selina and Himera, and also to Acragas, put fear into the people. It seemed to all of them that the terror of the Carthaginians had been conducted in their own sight. For none of those who were captured were spared, but, without showing compassion on those unlucky enough to be captured, they crucified some and led others into intolerable indignities.

Suetonius reports that Julius Caesar had the throats of certain pirates cut before they were crucified, so that they would not have to endure the full horror of such an execution.

Suetonius, Divus Julius 74[21]
The pirates, by whom he had been captured, were brought back under his control. Having sworn beforehand that he would crucify them, he first had their throats cut, and then did so.

1:26 **For consider your own calling, brothers and sisters: that not many of you were wise, humanly speaking; not many were powerful; not many were of noble ancestry.**

---

[19] This comes as part of a discussion of the assertion that the Scythians shun the practices of other countries.

[20] In context, Dionysius is warning people of the impending arrival of the warring Carthaginians.

[21] This is presented by Suetonius as an example of Caesar's relative gentleness in retaliation.

Consider your own calling

The location of Corinth contributed to its reputation for wealth and prosperity. In the middle of the first century, Corinth was one of the great centres of admiration for Rome. The city had been colonised by Rome, and remained a centre for those who admired, envied, or pursued Roman status and values, such as power, freedom, and wealth.[22]

> *Strabo: Geography, 8.6.20*[23]
> And Corinth is called wealthy on account of the trading station situated on the Isthmus; and is master of two harbours, one of which leads to Asia, and the nearby one to Italy . . .
> And also the Isthmian games were celebrated there, customarily drawing crowds . . .
> The temple of Aphrodite became wealthy in this way, so that it acquired more than a thousand temple slaves, *hetairas*, whom both men and women dedicated to the goddess. And on account of these the city expanded and became rich.

> *Strabo: Geography, 8.4.8*
> Corinth was razed [by the Romans] and then raised up again.

> *Pausanius, Description of Greece, 2.1.2*
> Now the Corinthians of Corinth are not of those of the older periods, but colonists sent by Rome.

> *Inscription at Roman Corinth: Latin; marble base, from time of Augustus*
> To G. Heius Aristo
> Aedile, Duovir, Duovir Quinquennalis
> Dedicated by
> The Colonists

The categories associated with "fortune" by Aristotle in the quotation below were still held to be natural associations by many in the first century:

---

[22] See, for example, Sophia B. Zoumbaki, 'The Composition of the Peloponnesian Elites in the Roman period and the Evolution of their Resistance and Approach to the Roman Rulers' *Tekmiria* 9 (2008), 25–52.

[23] Strabo's account appears to (hyperbolically) refer to Corinth before the Roman destruction, as Strabo goes on to describe his own visit to the city "after its recent reconstruction by the Romans" in 8.6.21.

Aristotle: Rhetoric 2.12.1–2[24]
We now come to consider different sorts of character, in terms of the emotions, habits, ages, and fortunes . . . With regard to "fortunes", I am talking about noble ancestry and wealth and power, and the opposites of these things, and generally, good or bad fortune.

The wording of Paul's exhortation to the Corinthians in this context may allude to the common biblical theme of reversal, in which God brings down the boastful rulers, but exalts his lowly, oppressed, weak people (cf. Josephus, *Antiquities*, 1.227):

Judith 9:11 . . . 14[25]
For your might is not in numbers, nor your power in the strong; but you are God of the humble, helper of the inferior, protector of the weak, shelterer of the weary, saviour of the despairing . . . And may you make your whole nation and every tribe know that you are God, God of all power and might, and that there is no other defender of the people of Israel except you!

Powerful
Aside from continuing the connotations of the stereotypical foolish ruler of Jewish wisdom literature, the word conjures the image of social influence, as illustrated in Philo's use of the same term:

Philo: Life of Moses, 1.49[26]
[A person fleeing from an angry king] might desire to come into the open and see if, through persistence, they gain the goodwill of people of power and utmost strength.

Noble Ancestry
One's status was not completely dependent on one's rank or ancestry; but these things were certainly influential and frequently a cause of boasting.[27]

---

[24] These elements of good fortune are assumed by Aristotle to be widely accepted.

[25] This is part of Judith's climactic prayer to God, pleading that he might bring about a reversal of fortunes.

[26] Philo is contrasting what a "normal" person might do in such a situation with what Moses did.

[27] See Bruce W. Winter, *Philo and Paul Among the Sophists: Alexandrian and Corinthian Responses to a Julio-Claudian Movement*, 2nd Ed. (Grand Rapids, Michigan/Cambridge, U.K., Eerdmans, 2002).

The first century Babbius Monument of Roman Corinth illustrates that Babbius was able to achieve a status that surpassed his rank as a freedman:

Dio Chrysostom protests against the sorts of categories that appear to have enamoured the Corinthians:

> *Dio Chrysostom: On Slavery and Freedom, 15.32*[28]
> Similarly, in relation to humans, one ought not to say that these ones are noble, or of noble ancestry, or free; or that those ones are of no ancestry, or poor, or slaves.

**1:27 But God chose the foolish things of the world in order to put to shame the wise; and God chose the weak things of the world in order to put to shame the
strong; 28 and God chose those of the world of no ancestry and the despised,
those that are not, in order to bring to nothing those that are, 29 so that no flesh
might boast before God. 30 It is from him that you are, in Christ Jesus, who became wisdom for us from God – that is, righteousness and sanctification and
redemption – 31 in order that, just as it is written: Let the one who boasts boast in the Lord.**

In order to bring to nothing
This word (καταργέω) is utilised at a number of points in the letter (1:28; 2:6; 6:13; 13:8; 13:10; 13:11; 15:24; 15:26), and seems to hint at the theme of reversal noted above. The related noun is used with a similar connotation in Aquila of Sinope's Koine edition of the Old Testament, in Psalm 44:9 (numbered as 45:9).

Christ Jesus, who became wisdom for us from God
At times, "Wisdom" is personified in the wisdom literature of Israel. See, for example, Proverbs 8–9 and Wisdom of Solomon 10.

Let the one who boasts boast in the Lord!
Bold and groundless self-praise was not encouraged in Roman society:

---

28 The protest comes in the form of an overheard conversation between a free man and a slave.

Plutarch: Moralia, 539d[29]
We regard those who praise themselves as shameless.

540b
Self-praise that arises from envy and jealousy of the praises of others should be well guarded against.

However, it is clear that Paul understands "boasting" as a theological category. As his adaptation of Jeremiah 9:23–4 (22–3 in Septuagint) illustrates, Jewish prophetic and wisdom literature makes a sharp distinction between dependently boasting in *humans* and dependently boasting in the *Lord*. It seems that Paul perceives the Corinthian church to be effectively doing the former rather than the latter:

Jeremiah 9:22–23, Septuagint
Thus says the Lord: "The wise should not boast in their wisdom, and the strong should not boast in their strength, and the wealthy should not boast in their wealth. But let the one who boasts boast in this: That they understand and know that I am the Lord, who makes mercy and justice and righteousness upon the earth, because these things are my will", says the Lord.

Sirach 1:11[30]
The fear of the Lord is glory and a boast and gladness and a crown of rejoicing.

Sirach 9:16
May righteous men be your dinner companions, and may your boast be in the fear of the Lord.

Sirach 10:19–22
What seed is honourable? Human seed. What seed is honourable? Those who fear the Lord. What seed is dishonourable? Human seed. What seed is dishonourable? Those who break the commandments. Among brothers and sisters, the one who leads them is honoured; but in the Lord's eyes, it is those who fear him. Wealthy or esteemed or poor, their boast is the fear of the Lord.

---

[29] This is part of a work in which Plutarch indicates how one might pursue appropriate and inoffensive self-praise (such as in the context of self-defence).

[30] This chapter sets up the book by emphasising that genuine wisdom necessarily comes from God – as can be seen in the subsequent quotations.

Sirach 11:1
The wisdom of the humble lifts their head, and they will sit in the midst of those who are great.

Pseudo-Phocylides: Sentences, 53–54[31]
Do not be arrogant with respect to wisdom or strength or wealth. The one God is wise, powerful, and at the same time full of blessing.

2:1 And in coming to you, brothers and sisters, I did not bring eminence of
speech or of wisdom as I proclaimed to you the mystery of God. 2 For I dec-
ided not to know anything among you except for Jesus Christ, and him cruci-
fied. 3 And I came to you in weakness and in fear and in much trembling, 4 and
my speech and my proclamation were not with the persuasions of wise words,
but with a demonstration of Spirit and of power, 5 in order that your faith
might not be in the wisdom of humans but in the power of God.

In coming to you
Acts 17–18 reports that Paul came to Corinth from Athens, where he had been appalled at the idols he saw in the city, and went on to address the Stoics and Epicureans at the Areopagus. Below is the Acropolis (left) and its views of the Temple of Olympian Zeus (middle) and the Theseum (right), all of which were present at the time of Paul's visit:

The *agora* and *stoa* of Athens:

[31] This occurs in a section about honesty and sincerity.

The steps and the rocky foundation that remains of the Areopagus

On his way from Athens to Corinth, Paul would have passed through Eleusis (50km east of Corinth), which was famous for its religious "mysteries" of Demeter and Persephone, in which initiates were guided by the priestesses into secret knowledge, ecstatic experience, and possibly the assurance of some sort of personal immortality. Roman Corinth had its own cult of Demeter and Persephone, with its own distinctive religious rites, located at the base of Acrocorinth. Roman lamps, pottery, and other finds from this site are numerous, dating from the mid-first century – the time that 1 Corinthians was written.[32] It was in the second century, however, that mystery cults became much more prominent. Eleusis (modern day Elefsina) and depictions of its rites can be seen below:

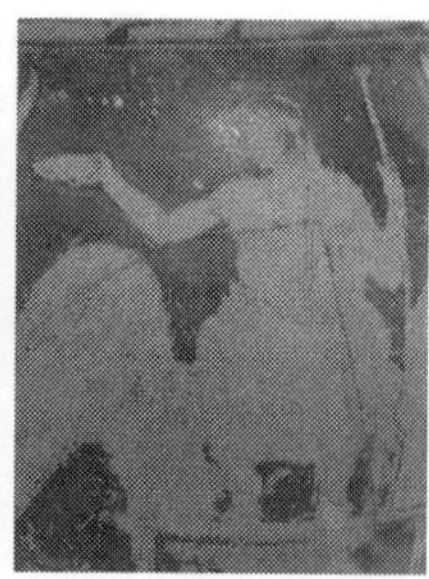

[32] See for example: Nancy Bookidis, "The Sanctuaries of Corinth" in Charles K. Williams II and Nancy Bookidis (eds), *Corinth: The Centenary 1896–1996* (The American School of Classical Studies at Athens, 2003).

Homeric-style Hymn to Demeter: Lines 480–482
Blessed among humans on earth is the one who has viewed these things [i.e. the rites and mysteries of Demeter]. But those who are uninitiated [that is, incomplete; immature; imperfect] in relation to the mysteries, who do not have a share, will not have a like apportionment when they have passed away to the realms of dank darkness.[33]

Demeter:

Corinth had ports on two seas. The "diolkos" (the grassy pavement below) provided a path over which boats had been dragged on wheels in well-known military expeditions:[34]

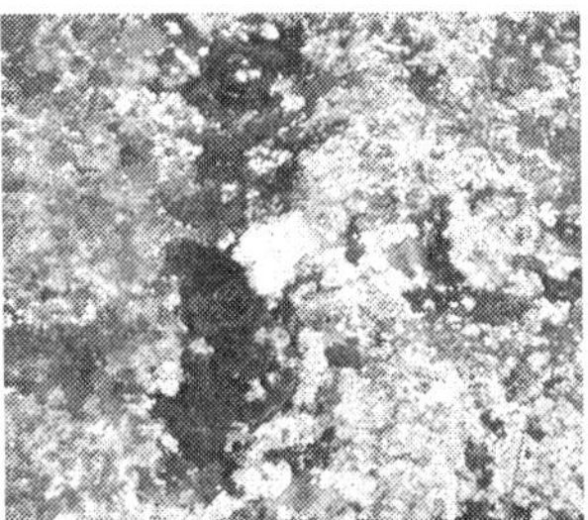

Strabo: Geography, 8.2.1
But the Isthmus, at the *diolkos*, which is the passage through which boats are hauled from one sea to the other, is forty stadia.

Pausanius: Description of Greece, 2.1.2
Now the Isthmus of the Corinthians stretches out on the one side toward Cenchreae, and on the other toward the Lechaion Sea.

Paul probably arrived at Corinth via the Lechaion Road:

[33] This section comes at the conclusion of the hymn.

[34] Although the *diolkos* is frequently mentioned by commentators and preachers as a thoroughfare for commercial exchange, it seems unlikely that the *diolkos* was used for commercial transfer across the isthmus. See David K. Pettegrew, "The Diolkos of Corinth," *American Journal of Archaeology* 115/4 (2011): 549–574.

He may have seen the pavement possibly installed by his Christian friend (cf. Romans 16:23), the politician (*aedile*) Erastus.[35] The Latin inscription can be seen below.

Inscription: Latin; limestone, East of stage building of Theatre; First Century?; pictured above
Erastus, for his aedileship,
at his own expense, laid [this pavement]

The Temple of Apollo was prominent in the city centre:

Below is the nearby Temple of Octavia, where the Roman imperial cult seems to have flourished:[36]

[35] This is highly debated. See, for example, Steven J. Friesen, "The Wrong Erastus: Ideology, Archaeology, and Exegesis," in Friesen, Schowalter, and Walters (eds.), *Corinth in Context: Comparative Studies on Religion and Society* (Leiden: Brill, 2010), 231–256.

[36] The location is more correctly referred to as "Temple E". On the institution of an Imperial Cult in Corinth in 54 CE see Anthonty J.S. Spawforth, "Corinth, Argos, and the Imperial Cult: Pseudo-Julian, Letters 198" *Hesperia* 63.2 (1944), 211–232.

Pausanius: Description of Greece, 2.3.1
In the middle of the *agora* is a bronze Athena. On its pedestal are wrought glorious Muses. And above the *agora* is the temple of Octavia the sister of Augustus, who ruled Rome after Caesar, the founder of present Corinth.

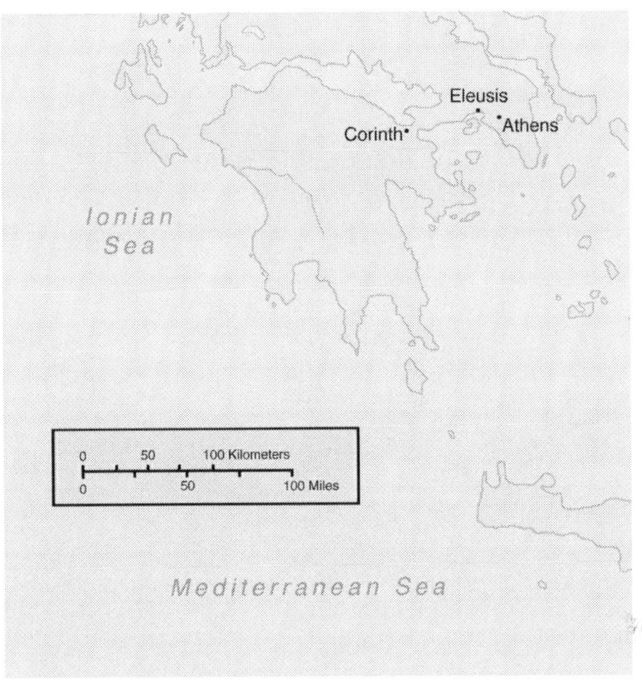

Eminence of Speech
The *Rhetorica Ad Herennium* recommends that the orator make use of a pleasing voice of "manly dignity", rather than "feminine exclamation" (3.12.22).

A demonstration of Spirit and of power
The term "demonstration" [ἀπόδειζις] is used ironically here, as it was known as a technical term of rhetorical "proof". See, for example, Cicero, *Academics*, 2.8; Quintilian, *Institutes of Oratory*, 5.10.7.

2:6–3:4: God's Spirit and Human Capability

2:6 But we speak wisdom among the mature – but a wisdom that is not of this age, nor of the rulers of this age, who are coming to nothing. 7 But we speak God's wisdom, in a mystery which has been hidden, which God fore-ordained before the ages for our glory, 8 which none of the rulers of this age has known.

For if they had known, they would not have crucified the Lord of glory. 9 But as it is written:

That which eye has not seen and ear has not heard, and which has not entered into the human heart
That which God has prepared for those who love him.

We speak wisdom among the mature
It is possible that Paul's use of words such as "mystery" and "mature" alludes to the bold claims of other philosophies or religions that had some influence in Corinth. Below is the ruined *telesterion* at Eleusis, where initiates had the "mysteries" of the gods revealed to them by the priestess, as illustrated in the wall relief:[37]

"Wisdom" was also a value of Paul's Hebrew heritage – and was understood as necessarily beginning with God himself (e.g. Job 12:13). Daniel 2:19 presents God as the one who reveals "mysteries" that would otherwise be impenetrable to the wisest of humans. The *Wisdom of Solomon* speaks similarly, insisting on the necessity of God's revelation for true wisdom:

> *Wisdom of Solomon 8:4*[38]
> For Wisdom is an initiate into the understanding of God, and an associate in his works.

---

[37] For the argument that 1 Corinthians reflects Paul's reaction against mystery-influenced Christianity, see Helmut Koester, *History & Literature of Early Christianity*, 2nd Edition (New York, Walter de Gruyter, 2000). It seems unlikely, however, that mystery religions were pervasive at this stage: See, for example, Hugo Rahner, *Greek Myths and Christian Mystery* (New York, Harper & Row Publishers, 1963).

[38] This is part of an extended section praising personified Wisdom.

Rulers of this age
Claudius (41 – 54 CE) was emperor at the time of Paul's stay in Corinth, and Nero (54 – 68 CE) had perhaps become emperor at the time that 1 Corinthians was written (53 – 55 CE). Their coins and statues can be seen below (Nero's coin and bust appearing on the left):

The following inscription illustrates the deification of Roman emperors after their deaths:

> *Inscription: Statue base, Sardis (41 – 54 CE)*
> To Tiberius Caesar,
> god
> Augustus
> the *imperator*, [uncle] of Tiberus
> Claudius
> Germanicus Caesar
> Ausgustus,
> the divine *imperator*
> and the
> city founder
> and benefactor of
> the world. Arising from piety
> and thanksgiving,
> the people
> have sanctified [this statue],
> the overseer of which has been
> Tib . . .

The phrase "rulers of this age", however, is broader than simply a reference to the emperor, and has theological significance. The reference appears to recall the figure of the foolishly ignorant opponent of God (and of God's people), developed in the psalms and literature of Judaism. Perhaps Paul sees some within the Corinthian church, in desiring observable wisdom and power, as unwittingly aligning themselves with the boastful "rulers of this age" (who will be condemned), rather than the crucified object of persecution (who will be vindicated).

The Psalms (eg. Psalm 2) and the book of Daniel (eg. Daniel 2–5) repeatedly present earthly "kings" and "rulers" as those who need to humbly learn that the "Most High" is sovereign. The theme is developed in other early Jewish literature:

> *Judith 8:16*[39]
> But you [rulers] do not control the decisions of the Lord our God, because God is not like a human, who can be threatened, or like human offspring, who can be bribed.

> *2 Maccabees 7:28–29*[40]
> "I beg you, child: Look up to heaven and to the earth, and see everything that is in them, and know that God did not create them out of existing things – and so it is also with the human race. Do not fear this executioner, but be worthy of your brothers in also accepting death, in order that in His mercy, I might receive you back along with your brothers."

The limitation of the dominion of these rulers to "this age" reminds of the apocalyptic distinction between the present (earthly) realm and the future (and heaven-controlled) realm. See comments in relation to 3:18.

The Lord of glory

The apocalyptic *Book of the Watchers* uses similar terminology when making an emphatic distinction between the destiny of "sinners" and the glorious Lord of the "righteous":

> *1 Enoch 22:13–14*[41]
> And this is what has been prepared for the spirits of those humans who are not godly but sinners, and who are partakers in lawless acts. And because their oppressions are punished there, their spirit will not be avenged on the day of judgement, nor will they be raised from that place. Then I blessed the Lord of glory, and said, "You are blessed, O Lord of righteousness who reigns forever!"

[39] Here Judith is rebuking the elders of the people for thinking that they could predict the time of God's help.

[40] In context, a mother is urging her tortured son not to fear the ruler who is about to kill him, but to trust that God will raise the righteous dead.

[41] This comes in the context of a vision of the underworld.

For Paul the distinctions in status are the opposite of what might be expected: The "Lord of glory" is apparently punished while the blind rulers continue to reign.

That which eye has not seen

The theme of seeing but not perceiving runs through much of Isaiah (6:9–10; 52:15; 64:4). It may be significant that the non-perceiving heart is characterised as "human", a term used throughout chapters 1–4, drawing on the prophetic designation of the world's rulers as "merely human" oppressors of God's people (e.g. Psalm 9:19–20).

**2:10 But to us, God has revealed this through the Spirit. For the Spirit searches everything, even the depths of God. 11 For who, among humans, knows the things of a person except the spirit of that person, which is in them? So also no one knows the things of God except the Spirit of God. 12 And we have not received the spirit of the world, but the Spirit that comes from God, in order that we might know the things that have been graciously given to us from God. 13 And that which we speak is not the teaching of human wise speech but the teaching of the Spirit, instructing those who are Spiritual with Spiritual things. 14 But the natural [ψυχικός] person does not receive the things of the Spirit of God. For they are foolish to such a person, who is not able to know them – because they are Spiritually [πνευματικῶς] discerned.
15 But the one who is Spiritual discerns all things, without being discerned by anyone.**

The depths of God

That God is unsearchable is a theme of the book of Job (e.g. 5:9; 9:4, 10; 11:7–9).

Those who are Spiritual

It seems that the designation "spiritual" was related to the competition for esteem among the Corinthian believers. In first century Roman society, the term "spirit" had some use in Stoic and other articulations of reality:

> *Seneca: Epistles, 41.1–2*[42]
> God is near you, with you, within you. This is what I am saying, Lucilius: A sacred spirit lies inside us; an observer of our good and bad deeds, and a protector. In accordance with the way we treat it, it treats us.

---

[42] This letter is about the importance of the human *soul* as a locus for the activity of the divine.

However, Paul refuses to remove the term from its relation to the Spirit of God, who is the means of divine revelation.

The Old Testament introduces certain figures as experiencing a special apportionment of God's Spirit, often related to divine revelation or enablement (e.g. Joseph: Genesis 41:38–9; Bezalel: Exodus 31:2–3; Moses: Numbers 11:17; Gideon: Judges 6:34). Acts 2:16–21 interprets the events of Jesus as bringing the promised age of God's Spirit.

The natural person

This word (ψυχικός) is notoriously difficult to interpret. In 4 Maccabees, it is used to distinguish "soulish" desires from "bodily" desires, both of which are in need of taming:

> *4 Maccabees 1:31–2*[43]
>
> It is moderation that rules over the desires. And of these desires, some are soulish [ψυχικαί] and others are bodily; and reason clearly rules over both of these.

Paul's use of the term is made somewhat accessible by that which he sets it against: Those who are ψυχικός are contrasted with those who are πνευματικός; that is, characterised by the Spirit of God.

2:16 For who has known the mind of the Lord;
in order to instruct him?

But we have the mind of Christ.

Who has known the mind of the Lord?

Jewish wisdom literature often emphasises that God cannot be directed or grasped by humans. God alone grants wisdom (Isaiah 40:13; cf. Daniel 2:22–3):

> *Wisdom of Solomon 9:13–14 . . . 17*[44]
>
> For what human can know the counsel of God? Or who can discern what the Lord wills? For the reasonings of mortals are worthless . . . But who has known your counsel, except the one to whom you have given wisdom, and to whom you have sent your holy spirit from above?

[43] See the comments on Plato's idea of the tripartite soul in relation to Excursus 5–14 and 15:32 for a similar conception. Here in 4 Maccabees, this verse comes to the heart of the central thesis.

[44] This comes as part of an extended section that praises personified wisdom.

Judith 8:12–14[45]

And now, who are you to put God to the test today, and to stand in place of God in the midst of humans? And now you are testing Almighty God, but you will never have knowledge. For you are not able to search out the depths of the human heart, and you are not able to access the thoughts of the human mind. So when it comes to God, who has made all of these things, how will you search out and come to know his mind, or come to understand his thinking?

3:1 But, brothers and sisters, I was not able to speak to you as to Spiritual people,
but rather as to those who are fleshly, as to infants in Christ. 2 I gave you milk to
drink, not food, for you were not able to receive it. And you are still not able – 3
because you are still fleshly. For where there is zeal and strife among you, are
you not fleshly, and walking as humans? 4 For when someone says, "I belong to
Paul", and another, "I belong to Apollos", are you not humans?

Infants in Christ

This is relatively common imagery, summoning hearers to grow up and leave childish ways behind (cf. Philo, *Every Good Man is Free*, 160):

Epictetus: Discourses, 2.16.25[46]

When little children cry at the nurse leaving them for a short time, they immediately forget their sadness upon receiving a cake. So do you want us to liken you to children? No, by Zeus! For it is not fitting for me to be pacified by this cake, but by right opinions.

2.16.39

Do you not wish to be weaned already, like children, and eat solid food, rather than crying for Mammas and nurses – the complaints of old women?

Philo: On Husbandry, 9[47]

And seeing as milk is food for infants, but cooked food is for the mature, so also there is milky nourishment for the soul, which is food for the time of childhood, in the form of the preschools of art. But then there are also mature foods for those who are grown men, in the form of guidance in wisdom and modesty and all virtue.

---

45 Here Judith is rebuking the elders of the people for thinking that they could predict the time of God's help.

46 The context is an argument about those who are too distracted to courageously align their will with that of God.

47 This comes in the context of a comparison of agricultural methods to "soul husbandry".

Are you not humans? . . . Let no one boast in humans!

Chapters 1–4 frequently pit that which is "human" against that which is "of God". It seems that, in continuity with the Old Testament prophets, Paul seeks to summon those whom he perceives as boastful and puffed up away from aligning themselves with the values and power of human rulers, and rather to trust in God, who will lift up the weak and humble.

Esther Addition C: 14:17e[48]

But I have done this [refused to bow down to Haman] in order that I might not place the glory of a human above the glory of God, and that I might not worship anyone besides you my Lord, and that I might not act in arrogance.

Sirach 42:18–20[49]

He [the Lord] seeks out both the depths and the heart, and he considers their crafty ways. For the Lord knows all that can be known, and he sees the signs of this age, announcing the things that have happened and those that will come, and revealing the steps that are hidden. No thought gets away from him, and not one word is hidden from him.

Philo, On the Decalogue, 4-6[50]

In cities, then, there also arises the greatest of all enemies, pride, which some admire and worship, making vain glories respectable through golden crowns and purple robes and an abundance of servants and carriages, on which these so-called blessed and happy ones are borne along . . . [exhibiting] exceeding pride. Pride is also a creator of many other evils: Boasting, conceit, inequality; and these are the sources of foreign and civil wars, allowing nothing to remain intact – nothing public or private, on land or on the sea. But why call to mind only those sins that are between people? For in pride also divine things are brought into contempt.

Philo, On the Decalogue, 41[51]

For if the One who is uncreated and imperishable and eternal, who needs nothing and is maker of everything, the Benefactor and king of kings and God of gods could not bring himself to overlook the humble . . . why should

---

[48] This is an expansion of the biblical story.

[49] This section (42:15–25) explores the glory of God the creator, who is beyond anything in all creation, whether human or angelic.

[50] Philo is answering the question of why Moses received the laws in the desert rather than in a city.

[51] Philo's emphasis in context is that God is willing to condescend to offer his laws to each individual.

I, as a mortal, carry myself in a way that is arrogant and puffed up and loud-mouthed toward those like myself?

Philo, The Special Laws 1.311[52]
Let God alone be your boast and greatest glory, rather than wealth or glory or rule or a well-formed body, or strength or similar things, to which the empty-minded customarily aspire.

Philo, On the Life of Moses, 1.30[53]
Therefore the many, even if only the briefest breeze of fortune should come their way, become puffed up and greatly inflated, bragging that those not in the limelight are scum [καθάρματα].

3:5–4:5: God's Work and Human Authority

3:5 What then is Apollos? And what is Paul? Servants, through whom you came to believe, and each as the Lord assigned to them: 6 I planted, Apollos watered, but God made it grow. 7 So neither the planter is anything, nor the waterer, but God the grower. 8 The one who plants and the one who waters are one, and each will receive their own reward, according to their own work. 9 For we are God's co-workers. You are God's field, God's building.

Servants . . . as the Lord assigned
It seems that Paul is at pains to distance himself and Apollos from competitive conventions of reciprocity that might otherwise be associated with travelling speakers. Seneca laments the fact that some people would only pursue virtue for the sake of commercial gain. Paul emphasises that it is *God* who repays his workers.

Seneca: On Benefits, 4.1.1–2[54]
[We are considering] whether the giving of benefits, and the esteem that is returned for them, are to be sought for their own sake. There are some who act with honour only for the reward, being unsatisfied with free virtue; although it carries no greatness if it is for sale!

52 Philo is considering God's gracious care of orphans and widows.

53 The point is that Moses scorned the life of luxury.

54 This is the beginning of a letter in which the Stoic Seneca insists that virtue is more at home in poverty than in payment.

You are God's field
Fields surrounding ancient Corinth, viewed from Acrocorinth:
A similar metaphor occurs in Isaiah 5, where Israel is pictured as a vineyard planted by God (cf. Ezekiel 36:9).

God's building
Herod's temple was still standing in Jerusalem at the time that 1 Corinthians was written. The Qumran community likewise used this imagery of themselves (1QS 8:5–10).

3:10 According to the grace of God that he gave me, I have laid a foundation as a wise master builder, and another has built on it. But let each watch how they build. 11 For no foundation is able to be laid other than that which has already been laid – which is Jesus Christ.

I have laid a foundation
Here Paul adapts a common image (cf. Hebrews 11:10):

> *Epictetus: 2.15.8*[55]
> What are you doing, man? It is not *all* assumptions, but *right* assumptions, that matter. If you feel that it is now night time, whatever it seems to you, do not change your mind, but keep your assumption, and say, "It is necessary to keep to one's assumptions!" But do you not want to securely set the beginning and foundation of your assumption – to see whether your judgement is sound or not sound, and thus build the rest of your construction well on this secure foundation? But if you have a rotten and unsafe

[55] Epictetus is developing an argument against those who hold onto untested assumptions.

undergirding, will your building not fall down – and all the more quickly if the materials that you place on it are substantial and strong?

Philo: On Dreams, 2.8[56]
Let us proceed to build on these foundations in the manner of the wise master builder, Allegory, following directions as we build.

More significantly, the image is used of an eschatologically restored temple in Isaiah 28:16.

3:12 And if anyone builds on the foundation with gold, silver, precious stones, wood, straw, or stubble, 13 the work of each will become clear, for the day will make it plain – because it will be revealed by fire. And the fire will test the quality of each one's work. 14 If someone's work, which they have built, remains, they will receive a reward. 15 If someone's work is burnt up, it will perish. The person, however, will be saved – but as if through fire. 16 Do you not know that together you are the temple of God, and that the Spirit of God dwells among you? 17 If someone destroys the temple of God, God will destroy that person. For the temple of God is holy, and that temple is you.

It will be revealed by fire
Stoicism held to a final conflagration, which would bring the universe back to its elements (with some possibility of renewal). The biblical prophets (Isaiah 33:11; Zechariah 13:9; Malachi 4:1) and early Judaism utilised the image of fire as a picture of testing:

Wisdom of Solomon 3:5–6[57]
And having been disciplined a little, they will be rewarded a lot, because God tested them, and found them to be worthy of himself. As gold in the furnace he refined them, and has received them as a whole burnt offering.

Testament of Abraham: Recension A, Chapter 13, lines 36–43[58]
[The archangel Puruel] tests the works of humans through fire. And if the fire burns up someone's work, immediately the angel of judgement takes that person and carries them to the place of sinners, a bitter place of correction. But if the fire tests someone's work and does not touch it, this per-

---

56 Philo is commenting on Joseph's interpretation of dreams.

57 This refers to the souls of the righteous, who had apparently died in disgrace.

58 This may well post-date 1 Corinthians. Abraham is depicted as foreseeing God's final judgement.

> son will be justified, and the angel of righteousness will take them and carry them to be saved in the inheritance of the righteous.

God dwells among you
The image of eschatological temple dwelling is utilised in Ezekiel 40–48, and is taken up in subsequent apocalyptic literature, including 1 Enoch 91 and 4QFlorilegium.

If someone destroys the temple of God, God will destroy that person
2 Samuel 6:1–11 tells the story of how Uzzah presumed to touch the ark, which was to become the centrepiece of the temple. According to verse 7, Uzzah was immediately destroyed by God.

3:18 Do not deceive yourselves: If any among you think of yourselves as wise in this age, you should become foolish, in order that you might become wise.
19 For the wisdom of this world is foolishness before God. For it is written:

The one who traps the wise in their craftiness

20 And again,

The Lord knows the reasonings of the wise, that they are useless.

21 So let no one boast in humans: For all things are yours – 22 whether Paul or Apollos or Cephas or the world or life or death or things present or things to come, all are yours; 23 and you are Christ's, and Christ is God's.

Wise in this age
The phrase "this age" expresses apocalyptic eschatology: those who seek esteem in the present age are bound to lose that esteem in the age to come. See also in the New Testament: Matthew 12:32; Luke 18:30; 20:34; 2 Corinthians 4:4; Ephesians 1:21.

Outside of the New Testament, this sort of "two-age" theology is evidenced in numerous apocalyptic works. The *Book of the Watchers* is illustrative of an expectation of sudden judgement that will usher in the new age:

> *1 Enoch 1:1 . . . 6–9*[59]
> The message of blessing from Enoch, with which he blessed the righteous elect who were to come in the day of crisis, when all the enemies would rise up – and the righteous would be saved . . .

[59] This is the beginning of the work, and introduces a fundamental apocalyptic orientation.

And they will be shaken and will tumble, and the highest mountain will be broken up, and the highest peaks of the protruding mountain will be brought low, and will melt like wax in front of a flaming fire. And the earth will be divided in a great rupture. And everything that is on the earth will be destroyed, and judgement will come upon all things. And as for the righteous, he will make peace, and there will be perseverance and peace upon the elect, and he will have mercy on them. And they will all belong to God, and he will give them contentment, and he will bless all. And he will be the helper of all, and will aid us, and provide them with light, and bring peace upon them. Because he is coming with his hosts and his holy ones, to bring judgement upon all, and to destroy all the ungodly, and to convict all flesh of all their works of ungodliness which they have committed, and the stubborn words that they have said, and all the things that the ungodly sinners have said against him.

The one who traps the wise . . . The Lord knows the reasonings of the wise
The former quotation is from Job 5:13 (cf. Jeremiah 8:9). The latter quotation adapts the Greek of Psalm 94:11 (93:11 in Septuagint):

Psalm 93:11, Septuagint
The Lord knows the reasonings of humans, that they are useless.

4:1 So, let people think of us as assistants [ὑπηρέτας] of Christ, and stewards of the mysteries of God.

Assistants of Christ
The *Wisdom of Solomon* uses the same term "assistants" to refer to kings, as those who have the task of acting under God's authority faithfully in relation to the people:

Wisdom of Solomon 6:4[60]
He will examine your works and will search out your plans, because as assistants [ὑπηρέται] of his kingdom you did not judge rightly.

4:2 Now it is desirable for stewards to be found faithful.

For stewards to be found faithful
The steward would look after the affairs of the master. Greek inscriptions sometimes apply the term to one who looked after a god such as Nike or

[60] This is a warning to the rulers who have persecuted the righteous people of God.

Artemis. The desirable attribute of faithfulness is illustrated in the honourable inscription "master-loving steward":

> *Inscription: Lakonike – Sparta (time of Antoninus Pius or Marcus Aurelius)*
> Guard of Everlasting Demea,
> Master-loving steward

4:3 But it is of the least consequence to me that I am judged by you or by any human judgement day. Rather I do not even judge myself. 4 For I am not aware of any wrongdoing, but I am not thereby vindicated. But the one who judges me is the Lord. 5 So let none of you judge before the time, until the Lord comes, who will illuminate the hidden things of the darkness, and will bring to light the desires of hearts; and then the praise will come to each from God.

The praise will come to each from God
Judgement and praise were significant issues in Roman culture. Certain innate attributes were generally considered honourable or praiseworthy – ancestry, gender, ethnicity; but these could be enhanced, destroyed, or bypassed by public actions that attracted praise or blame – such as benefaction or oratory.

> *Isocrates, To Demonicus, 1.33*[61]
> If there is anyone with whom you would like to become friends, you should speak well of them with those who will make it known. For praise is the beginning of friendship, while blame is the beginning of enmity.

The wise person's disregard of human judgements is a theme of Stoicism:

> *Diogenes Laertius: Lives of Eminent Philosophers, 7.117*[62]
> The wise person is said to be free of pride, for they accept both honour and dishonour equally.

However, Paul will not allow his apparent indifference to be interpreted in a Stoic manner; his reasoning is explicitly theological and eschatological. The Old Testament frequently pictures God as judge, and his final judgement as the "day of the Lord" (Isaiah 13:6; Ezekiel 13:5; Joel 1:15; Amos 5:18; Obadiah 1:15; Zephaniah 1:7; Malachi 4:5), when he would bring to light the things that had been hidden (Isaiah 29:15).

---

[61] This "moral treatise" (1.5) especially concerns the pursuit of quality friendships and virtuous character.

[62] This comes in a section about Zeno, the founder of Stoicism.

4:6–21: God's (Cruciform) Way and Human Boasting

4:6 These things, brothers and sisters, I have transformed [μετεσχημάτισα] so as to be simply about myself and Apollos, on your account. This is so that, through us, you might learn the meaning of "do not go beyond that which has been written, so that you will not become puffed up on behalf of one of us against the other. 7 For who differentiates you? What do you have that you did not receive? And if you received it, why do you boast as though you did not receive it?

I have transformed

Paul perhaps indicates here that he has made use of the Greco-Roman rhetorical device of *metaschematismos,* in which the real nature of the discussion is at first disguised, so as to allow a favourable hearing.[63] It may be debated whether the "disguise" here relates to the *personnel* (apparently Paul and Apollos, but actually Corinthian leaders) or the *application* (apparently the problem of strife relating to Paul and Apollos, but more fundamentally the theological problem of being puffed up).

4:8 Already you have become satisfied; already you have become rich; without us you have begun to reign! And I wish that you really had begun to reign, in order that we also might be reigning with you.

You have begun to reign

The belief that the people of God would share in a future reign, initiated by God, can be seen in Daniel 7:15–28.

Plutarch remarks, in *Tranquility of Mind* 472a, that Stoics were famous for desiring to be wise, just, strong, rhetorically competent, wealthy, and kingly (cf. Epictetus, *Discourses,* 3.22.95). Diogenes Laertius claims that the Stoics thought of themselves as, in a sense, godlike and priestly (*Lives of Eminent Philosophers,* 7.119). It may be that these sorts of values (to the extent that they were admired in Roman society in general) were influential on the Corinthian Christians.

4:9 For it seems to me that God has made a demonstration of us apostles as those who are last, as those condemned to die, because we have become a spectacle to the world and to angels and to humans. 10 We are fools on account of Christ – but you are wise in Christ! We are weak, but you are strong! You are honoured, but we are dishonoured! 11 Up to this very hour we both hunger and

---

63 See Hall, who draws on Chrysostom: David R. Hall, "A Disguise for the Wise: Metaschematismos in 1 Corinthians 4:6" NTS 40 (1984), 143–149; *The Unity of the Corinthian Correspondence* (London, T&T Clark/Continuum, 2003).

thirst, and go naked and beaten and homeless and persecuted, 12 and we labour, working with our own hands. 13 When reviled, we bless; when persecuted, we endure; when slandered, we encourage. We have become like the scum of the earth, the discarded filth of the world, right up until now.

Those condemned to die, a spectacle to the world

The same language is used in *Bel and the Dragon*, in the context of the familiar Jewish tale of reversal:

> *Bel and the Dragon 30–32*[64]
> And the king, seeing that a crowd of people had gathered together to press him, called his servants, and said, "Give Daniel over to be destroyed!" Now the den in which the lions were kept had seven lions, to which those who plotted against the king were handed over. And each day they fed them two bodies of those condemned to die. And the crowd threw Daniel into that den, in order that the lions might devour him, without the chance of a proper burial. And Daniel was in the den for six days.

At the theatres of Ancient Corinth, productions may have involved the figure of the "fool", and may have illuminated the image of being led to one's death. The larger (older) theatre seated 18,000:

The smaller "Odeion" was added in the first century

Wall decorations from the theatre:

[64] In this version of the story, the Babylonians believe that their king has become a Jew because of Daniel, so they force the king to have him killed.

Dio Chrysostom mentions, in passing, the Corinthian thrill at watching "those condemned to die":

> *Dio Chrysostom: The Rhodian Oration, 31.121*[65]
> So concerning the gladiatorial fights, the Athenians have so fiercely envied the Corinthians – or rather, have so surpassed them and all others in their possession by evil – that whereas the Corinthians watch these fights outside the city in a ravine, a place which is able to hold a multitude of people, but which otherwise is filthy and the sort of place where no one would want to bury a free person, the Athenians watch this fine sight in the theatre under the Acropolis!

The Arch of Titus in Rome, which, later in the first century, was to depict the humiliating Roman conquest of Jerusalem as a spectacle for the watching world:

Josephus describes the spectacle of this Roman victory in *Jewish War*, 7.132–57.

We are fools

The comic "fool" was a well-known character from Greek comedies. It may be that Paul is alluding to the comic shame associated with being a cosmic joke.

It would certainly have been a shameful thing for the Corinthians to have to think of themselves as followers of a fool – particularly one who conducted manual labour. The opening line of Aristophanes' play *Plutus* is illustrative:

> *Aristophanes: Plutus, Lines 1–2*[66]
> Cario [a slave]:
> How painful a thing it is, O Zeus and the gods,
> to be the slave of a foolish master.

---

[65] The point in context, of course, is about Athens. Corinth serves as a useful foil.

[66] Cario is complaining, because his master has decided to become a follower of a blind man.

You are honoured, but we are dishonoured
Paul seems to be drawing a distinction between the Roman-like triumphalistic aspirations of the Corinthians and the cross-like dedication of the apostles.

Aristotle expresses the all-important Greco-Roman regard for "honour", which was certainly still in place in Roman Corinth:

> *Aristotle: Nicomachean Ethics 4.3.17*[67]
> The great-souled person, then, is mostly concerned with honour and dishonour.

The following inscription reveals the competition for such honour in Greek religious associations:

> *Inscription: Delos (Second century* BCE*)*
> [Great honour, including gold crowns, is given to certain men for their contributions to a certain association]
> So that the others, seeing the apportionment of eternally-remembered honour to those good men, might become zealous for similar honours, and that they might be eager to enlarge the temple.

Philo, similarly to Paul, draws an ironic distinction between the "dishonoured" who are interested in virtue and the "honoured" who are interested only in themselves (cf. *Every Good Man is Free*, 6–11):

> *Philo: The Worse Attacks the Better, 34*[68]
> For those who are called lovers of virtue are almost all dishonoured, looked down upon, poor, lacking necessities, more dishonoured than both subject nations and slaves, filthy, pale, reduced to skeletons, looking around hungrily due to lack of food, subject to disease, in training for death. But those who look after themselves are honoured, wealthy, rulers, praised, given honour, healthy, fat, full of vigour, luxurious, corrupt, knowing no toil, familiar with pleasures which bear, through every sense, delights to the soul that receives everything.

---

[67] In context, the "great-souled" or "proud" person is presented as a man who claims much of himself, and is able to back up those claims. Aristotle presents such a person as a positive example. The pursuit of rightful honour is thus utterly noble.

[68] Lovers of "virtue" and of "self" are represented by Abel and Cain respectively.

Epictetus paints the Stoics as those who happily endure hardship (cf. Seneca, *Epistles*, 9.8–10; *On Benefits*, 4.2):

> *Epictetus, Discourses 2.19.24*[69]
> Show me someone who is sick and yet happy, endangered and yet happy, dying and yet happy, banished and yet happy, dishonoured and yet happy. Show me such a person: I desire, by the gods, to see a Stoic!

The scum of the earth
This may be an allusion to Lamentations 3:45 (cf. Nahum 3:6).

4:14 I do not write these things to shame you, but to warn you as my beloved children. 15 For even if you have plenty of "instructors" in Christ, you do not have many fathers.

Plenty of instructors
The "instructor" (παιδαγωγός) was a slave who aided a child. Such a person helped broadly with the child's educational upbringing:

> *Philo: On the Cherubim 71*[70]
> But if you allow yourself to be forever untrained [ἐπαιδαγωγητον] and untaught, you will be forever enslaved to tough mistresses, vague opinions, desires, pleasures, evils, follies, and false ideas.

It may be that Paul's terminology was ironic for those who considered themselves mature. As seen in the quotation from Diogenes Laertius below, "instructors" were those whose rule was limited to children:

> *Diogenes Laertius: Lives of Eminent Philosophers, 3.91–2*[71]
> Rule is divided into five parts: One relates to law, one relates to nature, one relates to custom, a fourth relates to birthright, and the fifth relates to might. Those in the cities take their right to rule from the citizens, and so rule according to law. Those who rule according to nature are males – not only among humans, but also among the other living creatures. For everywhere

---

69 Of course, a significant difference between the Stoic position evidenced by Epictetus and Paul's position here is that Paul expects eschatological vindication (cf. 4:8).

70 Philo is drawing a distinction between the recognition of God's ownership on the one hand, and slavery to lesser masters on the other hand.

71 Diogenes is outlining the views of Plato. Here he is pointing out that Plato liked to categorise things in sets.

the males rule to a great extent over the females. And those who rule according to custom are people such as instructors [παιδαγωγοί] of children and teachers of pupils. Those who rule according to birthright are people such as the Lakedemonian kings – for the kingdom is drawn from a particular family. And in Macedonia they rule in the same manner, for there the kingdom is also set by family. Others have forced or cheated their way into rule over cities. Their rule is known as being according to might. So rule is either according to law or nature or custom or birthright or might.

4:15 For in Christ Jesus I fathered you through the gospel. 16 I urge you then,
become imitators of me. 17 For this reason I have sent Timothy to you, who
is my beloved and faithful child in the Lord, and who will remind you of
my paths in Christ, just as I teach everywhere in every church. 18 Some of
you have become puffed up as though I were not coming to you. 19 But I will
come to you hastily if the Lord wills, and I will know not the speech of those
who have become puffed up, but their power. 20 For the kingdom of God is
not a matter of speech, but a matter of power. 21 What do you want – for me
to come to you with a rod, or in a spirit of love and gentleness?

Become imitators of me

The call to imitate a good example – particularly that of forefathers – is common in Greco-Roman literature. Paul's summons to become imitators of himself probably aims to include the "cross-like dedication" of the previous section.

Isocrates: Areopagiticus 7.84[72]

I have given these directions, that we might imitate the forefathers, and might thereby deliver ourselves of these evils and might become saviours not only of this city but also of all the Greeks.

Quintilian: Institutes of Oratory, 2.2.8[73]

However many examples for imitation he supplies from the readings, it will still be the so-called living voice that supplies them more fully, particularly if this is the voice of the teacher himself.

---

72 These are the closing words of the speech, urging listeners to respond in a way that will save Athens.

73 Quintilian is indicating the impact that the teacher of oratory will have upon students.

4 Maccabees 9:21–24[74]

And having already had the connection of his bones cut, the noble young man, worthy of Abraham, did not complain. But, as though transformed by the fire into an immortal state, he nobly endured the twisting of the wheel. "Imitate me, brothers!" he said. "Do not desert your post because of my struggle, or renounce the courageous brotherhood because of me! Fight the holy and noble battle for devotion to God, through which the righteous Knower of our ancestors might become favourable to our nation and punish the accursed tyrant!"

With a rod

This may be continuing the image of fatherhood from 4:15, hinting at the "rod of correction" seen in the Old Testament (e.g. Proverbs 10:13; 22:15).

[74] This is part of a vivid description of the willingness of seven young brothers to be tortured rather than give up obedience to the law and to Moses.

The Cross Applied I: Your Body Belongs to the Lord

Excursus: Chapters 5–14 and Pauline Ethics

Here the letter moves into an extended ethical section, which continues until the end of chapter 14.

The ordering of topics within this ethical section seems to follow a general pattern of Pauline ethics. It seems possible to detect a common movement of concepts within Paul's logic of sin/sanctification as follows:

- Theme I: Sanctification of the church that involves avoidance of sexual immorality, impurity, and greed/passionate desire – in relation to *bodies*[75]
- Theme II: Sanctification of the church that involves the avoidance of inter-relational sin, and the promotion of love – particularly expressed in self-restraint/submission within the *body* of Christ

This can be seen in the ethical sections and catechetical lists below, ordered approximately chronologically:

1 Thessalonians 4:
4:1–8: Theme I: Sexual immorality, bodies, lustful passions, greed
4:9–12: Theme II: Love

Galatians 5:
5:19–21ff: Theme I: Sexual immorality, impurity, debauchery, etc.
5:22–3: Theme II: Love, joy, peace, etc.

[75] The terminology of "body" is not always present, although it is these topics that Paul most frequently associates with such terminology. It may be that the unifying idea in *Theme I* is that of desiring and pursuing the forbidden.

2 Corinthians 12:20–21:
12:20: Theme II: Strife, zeal, evil speech, etc.
12:21: Theme I: (Former) impurity, sexual immorality, debauchery

Romans 1:
1:24: Theme I: Lusts, impurity, bodies
1:28–31: Theme II: "All" unrighteousness: Strife, deceit, etc.

Romans 12–15:
12:1–2: Theme I: Bodies devoted to God
12:3–15:33: Theme II: Love, concern for the other, one body

Colossians 3–4:
3:5–7: Theme I: Sexual immorality, impurity, evil lusts, greed, idolatry
3:8–4:1: Theme II: Wrath, evil speech; love; one body

Ephesians 2:
2:1–10: Theme I: Lusts of flesh, confronted with death & resurrection in Christ
2:11–22: Theme II: Division, confronted with death & resurrection in Christ; one body

Ephesians 4–6:
4:1–16: Theme II: Bear with one another in love. There is one body
4:17–24: Theme I: Gentiles have given themselves over to sensuality, impurity, greed
4:25–5:2: Theme II: Build each other up in love, being members of one another
5:3–14: Theme I: Among you there must not be even a hint of sexual immorality, impurity, greed
5:15–6:9: Theme II: Live wisely, filled with the Spirit, submitting to one another

The main ethical section of 1 Corinthians appears to follow a similar pattern. Chapters 5–7 deal especially with the issues of πορνεία (sexual immorality), πλεονεξία (greed), and καθαρσία (impurity) in relation to personal bodies. Chapters 8–14 are introduced with the maxim "love builds up", which may be heard to summarise the collected issues of that section, in which the Corinthian believers are called to forgo their own rights and freedoms within the body of Christ.

It is arguable that this pattern of ethical arrangement is Paul's Christocentric development of the ethical model that he had inherited from his "former life in Judaism" (Gal. 1:13) as a Pharisee. In particular, four related features of ethical arrangement in relevant works of the Hellenistic-Roman period are worthy of note:

1. An emphasis on the fundamentality of (idolatrous) sexual immorality, greed and impurity
2. The latter placement of discussion of sins of interpersonal social interaction
3. A logic in which the internal must precede the external
4. A logic in which the behaviour of the individual goes on to affect the community

These are by no means to be thought of as universal rhetorical rules, but rather recurring features found within a range of relevant literature:

1. An Emphasis on the Fundamentality of (Idolatrous) Sexual Immorality, Greed and Impurity

It is worth noting firstly that, in terms of Greek ethical reflection, ***Plato*** had influentially presented the "appetites" or "passions" for sex and food as being the basest expressions of human desire, which need to be controlled by "reason":

> *Plato: Republic, 4.439d*[76]
> We shall think that these things are twofold and different to one another: The one which reasons in the soul we call rationality; and the other which loves and hungers and thirsts, and concerning the other desires feels disturbance, we call the irrational and appetitive, companion of various fulfilments and pleasures.

The ethics of this tradition disapproved of unrestrained desire for the pleasures of sex and food, seeing such slavery to appetite as unfitting for the virtuous. ***Demosthenes***' assumptions about virtue and pleasure are illustrative of convention:

> *Demosthenes: 60.2 "Funeral Speech"*[77]
> For knowing that with good men, the needs of acquisitions and the enjoyments of the pleasures of life are looked down upon, but rather their whole desire is for virtue and praises…

[76] This is part of an argument that develops a view of the soul as tripartite, consisting of rational, spirited, and appetitive parts.

[77] This is the beginning of a speech in which Demosthenes honours those who have given their lives in battle.

A comparison of the ***Decalogue*** in Exodus 20 of the Hebrew and Greek texts reveals that the ordering of the second table has been rearranged in the Septuagint translation of the Hebrew Scriptures, moving the prohibition of adultery to a place of priority:

	Masoretic Text	Septuagint
1.	No other gods	No other gods
2.	No idols	No idols
3.	Using the name of the LORD	Using the name of the LORD
4.	Keeping Sabbath	Keeping Sabbath
5.	Honouring father & mother	Honouring father & mother
6.	**No murder**	**No adultery**
7.	**No adultery**	**No stealing**
8.	**No stealing**	**No murder**
9.	No false witness	No false witness
10.	No coveting	No coveting

Philo later makes much of this fact that the second table of the Decalogue (as seen in the Septuagint above) begins with the prohibition of sexual sin, a vice of "pleasure" that he takes to be universally fundamental:

> *Philo: On the Decalogue, 121–123*[78]
> And having wisely given these words concerning the honour of parents, he brings to an end the other "divine" set of five. In writing the other set, concerning prohibitions related to humans, he begins with adultery, taking this to be the greatest of crimes. For firstly it springs from the love of pleasure, which both enfeebles the bodies of those it holds, and loosens the tendons of the soul and destroys the very existence, consuming all that it touches as an unquenchable fire, leaving nothing safe in human life.

> *Philo: On the Decalogue, 168–169*[79]
> And the first set, each having the form of a summary, contains these five; while the special laws are not few in number. In the other set [i.e. the second table of commandments] the first heading is against adultery, under which come many directions: against corrupters, against pederasty, against lustful living, participating both in unlawful intercourse and licentious defilement.

---

[78] Philo is summarising the two "sets" of five commandments.

[79] Here Philo moves from discussing the first set of five commandments to discussing the second set.

Philo: The Special Laws 3, 8[80]
In the second tablet, the first commandment is this: "Do not commit adultery", because, I think, everywhere in the inhabited world, pleasure is a great force, and no part has escaped its domination.

A prayer in ***Sirach*** illustrates the way in which appetites for food and sex became thought of as fundamental vices to avoid:

Sirach 23:4–6[81]
O Lord, Father and God of my life, do not give me conceited eyes, and turn lust away from me. Do not let the desires of the belly and intercourse overpower me, and do not give me over to a shameless soul.

Pseudo-Eupolemus presents Abraham's piety as resulting in him being above greed and beyond the reach of sexual sin:

Pseudo-Eupolemus: Fragment 1, 3–7[82]
Having pursued piety, Abraham was pleasing to God....
When the elders came to him, suggesting that he might receive wealth in order to release the prisoners, he did not choose to take advantage of the unfortunate. But, having taken food for his young men, he returned the spoils....
Further, he reported that the king was not able to have intercourse with Abraham's wife, and that his people and household were perishing.

The book of ***Jubilees*** closely links both (Gentile-like) idolatry and (Gentile-like) sexual immorality with impurity: idols themselves are impure, and thus need to be avoided (11:4, 15–16; 20:7; 21:5); and sexual immorality (even when committed by an individual) could bring defilement to Israel as a whole (4:22; 7:27; 16:5–6; 20:3–6; 25:1; 25:7; 30:13–15; 33:7; 33:10–11; 33:20; 35:14; 41:17; 41:25–26). This emphasis on the necessity of purity is a feature of much Jewish literature subsequent to the events associated with the Maccabean revolt against the Hellenisation of Antiochus Epiphanes.

---

80 Philo is attempting to relate different sets of commands to one another.

81 This is presented as a prayer to the one who has the power to discipline the mind and discern sin.

82 Not much of the original context of this fragment survives. It seems that the author is pointing out the virtues that would have been applauded as pious. This version clearly differs from the Biblical account.

Jubilees 16:5[83]
All of their works are wicked and they are great sinners, making themselves unclean and enacting immoralities in their flesh, and accomplishing abominations throughout the land.

Jubilees 20:7[84]
And therefore I charge you, my sons: Love the God of heaven, and adhere to all of his commands. And refuse to go after all their idols and all their impurities.

The ***Wisdom of Solomon*** frequently depicts sexual immorality as a fundamental vice, and views sexual immorality and other sins as arising from idolatry:

Wisdom of Solomon 14:12[85]
For the idea of idols was the beginning of sexual immorality, and their invention was the corruption of life.

This sexual immorality connected to false religion may also be characterised as impurity, as in *Jubilees*:

Wisdom of Solomon 14:22–7[86]
It was not enough for them to stray concerning the knowledge of God, but also, living in great conflict due to ignorance, they call such evils peace! For, killing their children in sacrifice, or celebrating mysteries, or leading frenzies of strange rituals, they are pure neither in life nor marriage. Yet they lie in wait for one another in ambush or cause one another distress by committing adultery.

Book 3 of the Sibylline Oracles appears to conceive of the chief vices of the nations as arrogant greed and sexual immorality – at times connected with false worship:[87]

---

[83] This is a summary of the sin of Sodom.

[84] Abraham is teaching Ishmael, Keturah, Isaac, and their children. The verse cited is representative of his whole teaching in this context.

[85] This is part of a section that condemns the absurdity of idol worship.

[86] In context, this is presented as the result of a commitment to idolatry.

[87] Buitenwerf suggests that the chief vices in Book III are greed (avarice) and fornication. John J. Collins suggests that the chief vices in Book III are idolatry, greed, and fornication: John J. Collins, *The Apocalyptic Imagination: An Introduction to Jewish Apocalyptic Literature,* Second Edition (Grand Rapids, Michigan, Eerdmans, 1984, 1998), 123.

Sibylline Oracles: 3. 762–766[88]
But enliven your thinking in your breasts,
Flee unlawful worship, worship the living one.
Guard against adultery and homosexual intercourse.
Nourish and do not murder the children you have borne.
For the immortal one will become angry at the one who sins in these things.

The book of ***4 Maccabees***, clearly reminiscent of a Platonic evaluation of the passions, presents an argument for the control of the desires for (firstly) sex and food, by reason:

4 Maccabees 1:1 . . . 3–4[89]
Godly reason is master of the passions....
If therefore it is plain that reason can master those passions that hinder self-control, gluttony and lust, then it will also become evident that it is able to rule those passions that hold back justice, such as malice; and those passions that hold back courage, such as suffering and fear and pain.

The ***Testaments of the Twelve Patriarchs*** present sexual immorality and greed as the chief expressions of sin against God. These foundational vices are occasionally explicitly linked to idolatry and impurity. It is largely agreed that the Testaments as we currently have them evidence a degree of Christian influence. It is also largely agreed that they express continuity with Jewish ethical argumentation, and so it is interesting to see a continuation of a number of the ethical traditions examined so far:

Testament of Reuben, 4.6[90]
For sexual immorality is the destruction of the soul, separating it from God and bringing it near to idols.

Testament of Judah, 18[91]
Also I have read, in the books of Enoch the righteous, of the sorts of evil that you will do in the last days. Guard yourselves then, my children, from sexual immorality and from the love of money; listen to Judah your father,

[88] This occurs as an admonition that interrupts the oracles of judgement.
[89] This opening section explicitly sets up the theme as a philosophical one.
[90] The *Testament of Reuben* is first of the twelve, and introduces many of the themes of the collection. This Testament is summarised as concerning "thoughts", and this section deals especially with sexual immorality.
[91] The *Testament of Judah* is summarised as being about "courage and the love of money and sexual immorality".

because these things remove you from the law of God, and blind the understanding of the soul, and teach arrogance, and do not allow a person to show mercy to their neighbour, and deprive their soul of all goodness, and hold them in toils and labours, and take away their sleep, and waste away their flesh, and hinder the sacrifices of God, and do not allow recollection of blessing or obedience to the voice of prophecy, and cause one to be furious at the word of godliness. For one who is enslaved to these two passions before the commands of God cannot obey God, because the passions have blinded that person's soul, making them go about during the day as though it is night.

Testament of Dan, 5.6–8[92]
For I have read in the book of Enoch the righteous that your ruler is Satan, and that all of the spirits of sexual immorality and of arrogance will be subject to Levi, to trap the sons of Levi, making them sin before the Lord. And my sons will come near to Levi and sin with them in everything. And the sons of Judah will be caught up in greed, swindling the others as lions. On account of this, you will be led away together with them, into captivity, and there you will be inflicted with all of the plagues of Egypt and all of the wickedness of the Gentiles.

2. The Latter Placement of Discussion of Sins of Interpersonal Social Interaction

The fundamental vices identified above are not infrequently presented prior to vices of social interaction.

As mentioned above, ***Book 3 of the Sibylline Oracles*** pictures the chief vices of the nations as arrogant greed and sexual immorality. Sometimes these vices are portrayed as giving way to interpersonal havoc. Book 3.175–193 provides a useful example: The arrogance of the nations results immediately in a craving for impiety among them, involving homosexual sex. The ensuing affliction may be said to arise from shameful greed and ill-gotten wealth, and has the effect of stirring up interpersonal strife, in the form of hatred and deceit:

[92] The *Testament of Dan* is summarised as concerning "anger and lying". The figures of Levi (representing priesthood) and Judah (representing royalty) are prominent throughout the *Testaments*.

Sibylline Oracles: 3. 182–191[93]
And they will oppress mortals. But for those people there will be a great fall, when they begin their unrighteous arrogance. And among them will develop a compulsion for impiety, and men will have intercourse with men, and they will put children in shameful brothels. And a great distress will come to those people, and bring everything into confusion, and cut everything up and fill everything with evils, in shameful greed and ill-gotten wealth – in many areas, but mostly in Macedonia. And hatred will arise, and every sort of deceit will be among them.

Verses 3–8 of the ***Sentences of Pseudo-Phocylides*** may be viewed as an attempt to summarise the Decalogue.[94] This summary prioritises sexual sin, placing such vice prior even to respect for parents and God. Sexual sin, impurity, and the unjust accumulation of wealth are prominent in close proximity to one another. Stealing, lying, and honouring others are placed subsequently:

Pseudo-Phocylides: Sentences, 3–8[95]
Do not commit adultery, nor stir homosexual passion.
Do not sew together deceit, nor defile your hands with blood.
Do not become wealthy unjustly, but live from honourable means.
Be content with your possessions and abstain from those of another.
Do not tell lies, but always speak truth.
First honour God, and thereafter your parents.

In the ***Gospel of Mark*** Jesus is presented as illustrating the way in which a person is made impure by listing the sorts of sins that proceed from within. Once again there appears to be a general movement from vices including sex and greed to vices of social interaction:

Mark 7:20–23
He said, "It is that which comes out of a person that defiles the person. For from the heart of the person proceed evil thoughts, sexual immorality, theft, murder, adultery, greed, wickedness, deceit, debauchery, envy, slander, arrogance, foolishness. All these evils come from within and make a person unclean."

---

[93] This is presented as an oracle of judgement against the "kingdom" from the "western sea", arising after the rule of the Greeks and Macedonians – presumably, Rome.

[94] See P.W. Van der Horst, *The Sentences of Pseudo-Phocylides with Introduction and Commentary* (Leiden, Brill, 1978), 112.

[95] These verses follow immediately from the introductory prologue.

When the Synoptic Gospels present Jesus as being asked to list the commands of God, he lists the commands of the second table of the Decalogue, appending the command to honour father and mother. ***Luke*** alters the ordering of Matthew and Mark (where murder begins the list) to prioritise the prohibition of adultery, perhaps in order to keep to the ordering of the Septuagint:

> *Luke 18:20*
> You know the commands: Do not commit adultery, do not murder, do not steal, do not bear false witness, honour your father and mother.

This ordering thus reminds of the *Sentences* of Pseudo-Phocylides, 3–8 above.

Josephus' discussion of the law in *Against Apion* loosely follows the ordering of the Decalogue in the Septuagint, placing the discussion of sexual laws immediately after the laws related to God and Temple, and prior to discussion of laws relating to the interactional issues of honouring parents, lying, and stealing. As in Philo, Pseudo-Phocylides and Paul, sexual and family issues are combined. In summary:

> *Josephus: Against Apion, 2.190–208*
>
> 1. (2.190ff): God – creator; no images may be made; responded to with the worship of virtue
> 2. (2.193ff): Temple – priesthood; sacrifices; laws; prayers; fellowship; purifications
> 3. (2.199ff): Marriage/Sex – man and wife; homosexual sex; getting married; submission; assault/adultery; abortion; purifications; Children – sobriety in upbringing, education, moral grounding; The Dead – funerals
> 4. (2.206): Honouring Parents – second to honouring God; respect to elders
> 5. (2.207): Lying – no secrets; confidence; no bribes
> 6. (2.208): Stealing – taking goods, laying hands on neighbour's property; taking interest
> "These and many similar regulations are the ties that bind us together."

Josephus' discussion of the penalties prescribed by the law in the same work follows a similar order:

> 1. Sexual crime
> 2. Fraud/stealing
> 3. Dishonouring parents
> 4. Impiety toward God

Josephus viewed the Greek philosophers as having drawn on Moses to commend the dual themes of (individual) *simplicity of life* and (corporate) *fellowship with one another*:

> *Josephus: Against Apion, 2.281*[96]
> For first of these were the Greek philosophers, for whom it seemed that they observed their forefathers; but who in deeds and in philosophy followed that one [i.e. Moses], similarly thinking about God, and teaching simplicity of life and fellowship with one another.

At a number of points in the ***Testaments of the Twelve Patriarchs***, it is clear that the fundamental vices of greed and sexual immorality precede vices of social interaction:[97]

> *Testament of Reuben, 3.3–7*[98]
> First [of the spirits of error], the spirit of sexual immorality dwells in the nature and in the senses. Second, the spirit of greed, in the stomach. Third, the spirit of fighting, in the liver and the gall. Fourth, the spirit of flattery and trickery, in order that through meddling a person might appear seasonable. Fifth, the spirit of arrogance, in order that a person might be boastful and high-minded. Sixth, the spirit of falsehood, with destruction and jealousy, to fake words and conceal words from family and friends. Seventh, the spirit of injustice, with which come stealing and profiteering, in order that a person might achieve the pleasures of their heart. For the spirit of injustice works together with the other spirits, through bribery. On top of all of these is the spirit of sleep, the eighth spirit, which comes together with deception and fantasy.

> *Testament of Benjamin 6.1–6*[99]
> The mind of the good person is not in the hand of the spirit of deception, Beliar. For the angel of peace guides their soul. They do not look

---

[96] Josephus is arguing that the persistence of Judaism over time is evidence of its worthiness.

[97] On ordering within ethical lists of the Twelve Patriarchs, as well as Pseudo-Phocylides, Josephus, Philo, and other works, see Karl-Wilhelm Niebuhr, *Gesetz und Paränese: Katechismusartige Weisungsreihen in der frühjüdischen Literatur* (Tübingen, Mohr Siebeck, 1987).

[98] These seven "spirits of error" seem to be presented as a reversal of God's good order of creation: sexuality is depicted as the last element of divine ordering, but the first spirit of error, and so on.

[99] The *Testament of Benjamin* concludes and sums up the concerns of the *Twelve Patriarchs*, under the heading of a "pure mind".

passionately at perishable things, or gather wealth for the love of pleasure. They do not delight in pleasure, or grieve their neighbour, or fill themselves with food. They do not stray into the superficialities of what is seen, for the Lord is their portion. The good mind does not wait on the praise or dishonour of humans, and does not know any deceit or falsehood or fighting or reviling, for the Lord dwells in it and enlightens its soul; and it rejoices with all people at all times.

3. A Logic in which the Internal Must Precede the External

Plutarch indicates that the movement from dealing *firstly* with the soul's preoccupation with passion and greedy desire to dealing *secondly* with external matters (as seen in the above two sections) is not to be thought of as arbitrary. Rather, this ordering is essential for ethical success. Plutarch reasons:

> *Plutarch, Moralia* 100, "Virtue and Vice," 1
> The pleasant and happy life does not come from that which is external, but rather, the person who draws these things from their own character, as from a well, adds pleasure and joy to the things around them.

Therefore, it is essential that reason must first deal with the soul's tendencies toward passion and greed, before one can expect to deal appropriately with external things. Drawing on Plato, Plutarch asserts that at the most secret level, the soul inclines toward unrestrained fornication, greed, and lawlessness:

> *Plutarch, Moralia* 101, "Virtue and Vice," 2
> "For it [that is, vice] attempts sex with one's family," as Plato says, and seizes unlawful foods, and holds back from nothing.

Reason must therefore bring these carnal desires into line, if one is to expect any ethical development. Echoing Stoic sentiments, Plutarch insists that attempts at development will be fruitless, "unless you throw down the passions of the soul and put a cease to greedy desire, and escape from your fears and anxieties".[100] It is only once such base desires have been corrected by reason that external issues may become relevant.

[100] Plutarch, *Moralia* 101, "Virtue and Vice," 4.

4. A Logic in which the Behaviour of the Individual Goes on to Affect the Community

In a number of works that reflect on the Maccabean revolt against Antiochus Epiphanes in the 160s BCE, there is a logic in which the actions of a special few affect the wellbeing of the entire community.

The following examples from ***1 Maccabees, 2 Maccabees*** and the later ***4 Maccabees*** show that the special few who act in zeal, purity and righteousness may bring about the purity of the whole nation.

> *1 Maccabees 3:8*
> And [Judas Maccabeus] went through the cities of Judah and destroyed the ungodly out of Judah, and turned wrath from Israel.
>
> *2 Maccabees 5:27*
> But Judas Maccabeus, and a handful who had come with him, withdrew into the desert, and he survived in the manner of the wild animals in the mountains, together with those who were with him; and they continued to live on the nourishment of vegetation, so that they would not share in the defilement.
>
> *4 Maccabees 1:11*
> For it was not only the people in general who were amazed at their courage and endurance, but also those who were doing the torturing, as they were the cause that brought down the tyranny against the nation, having conquered the tyrant by their endurance, so that through them the homeland was purified.

This motif of the impact of the *special few* on the *nation* was further democratised by those who inherited the Judaism bequeathed by the Maccabean successes. The action of *every* individual in responding to the Torah became effective in a way that was comparable to Maccabean zeal.

From the perspective of the Pharisees, the adherence of individuals to the Torah and the traditions, and their avoidance of Gentile idolatry, affected the purity of the nation as a whole.[101]

---

[101] On the nature of the Pharisees as an influential group pushing for national reform, see Roland Deines, "The Pharisees Between 'Judaisms' and 'Common Judaism'" in Carson, O'Brien, and Seifrid (eds), *Justification and Variegated Nomism*, Vol.1 (Tübingen, Mohr Siebeck, 2001), 443–504; 461. See also Deines,

The ***Psalms of Solomon*** arguably express this Pharisaic perspective.[102] In a number of these Psalms, it seems that the judgement of God that has come upon Jerusalem is interpreted as being due to the Gentile-like immorality of individuals.

Psalms of Solomon 2:11–16
They [i.e. the Gentiles] held up the sons of Jerusalem to ridicule,
because of the prostitutes among her.
Every passer-by
entered in to them in broad daylight.
They [the Gentiles] mocked their lawless ways
compared to their own doings.
In broad daylight they displayed
their evil deeds.
And the daughters of Jerusalem are polluted according to your judgement.
For they defiled themselves in promiscuous disorder.
My stomach and my innards are sick because of this.
I will justify you, O God, with an upright heart,
because in your judgements there is justice, O God,
because you have repaid sinners according to their works,
according to their exceedingly wicked sins.

But the general logic of a relationship between individual behaviour and communal health is not only to be found in works associated with the Pharisees. In ***Philo's*** *On the Virtues*, 34–50, he pictures "the Hebrews" as those who are marked by monotheism and consequent mutual love. Their enemies realise that if the Hebrews can be enticed to sexual immorality and idolatry, their mutual love will have lost its foundation, and will fall apart. The enemies act on this insight and find some success, before those Hebrews of greater virtue (the vast majority) retaliate and find ultimate victory. It is clear for Philo that the pursuit of personal (particularly sexual) virtue and the avoidance of idolatry directly affect corporate mutuality and peace. He concludes:

"Pharisäer" in Coenen, Lothar, and Haacker, Klaus, *Theologishes Begriffslexikonzum Neuen Testament: neubearbeite Ausgabe, Band II* (R. Brockhaus Verlag Wuppertal, 2000), 1455–1468; 1461.

102 For the association of the Psalms of Solomon with the Pharisees, see, for example, Mikael Winninge, *Sinners and the Righteous: A Comparative Study of the Psalms of Solomon and Paul's Letters* (Uppsala, Almqvist & Wiksell International, 1995).

Philo: On the Virtues, 47
Therefore, Moses says in the Exhortations, "If you should pursue righteousness and godliness and the other virtues, you will live a life free of war and in uniform peace."

It may be, then, that these broad contours of ethical discussion in the period around the time of Paul are reflected in Paul's own ordering of ethical sections. For Paul, however, this pattern of ethical ordering has received a new focus: It evidences identification with *Christ*, who died and rose "in his body of flesh" (Colossians 1:22). Coming to him in faith, Christian assemblies are to turn from the desire for forbidden bodily pursuits (that is, sexual immorality, greed, and impurity), and join together as the unified body of Christ (in mutual love).

5:1–7:40: Sexual Immorality and Greed

5:1 It is actually said that among you there is sexual immorality, and such a type of sexual immorality that is not heard of among the Gentiles – so that someone has the wife of his father. 2 And you are puffed up!

Among you there is sexual immorality . . . not heard of among the Gentiles
This particular expression of *porneia* is viewed as beyond even that of the Gentiles. Perhaps drawing on Leviticus 18:6–8, *Pseudo-Phocylides* explicitly prohibits this sort of relationship.

Pseudo-Phocylides: Sentences, 175–180[103]
Do not remain unmarried, in order that you might not depart nameless.
Give to nature an offering: Bear children in turn, as you were given birth to.
Do not prostitute your spouse, defiling your children,
for the adulterous bed does not produce children in your likeness.
Do not touch your stepmother, the second wife of your father,
but honour her as a mother, as she walks in the footsteps of your mother.

Philo views this sort of relationship as scandalous:

[103] In this section of the Sentences, Pseudo-Phocylides goes through a number of family relationships, urging appropriate piety.

Philo: The Special Laws, III 14[104]
But what could be more ungodly than this wicked act? A father's deathbed, which should be left untouched as a guarded sacred stronghold, is disgraced, and an aging mother receives no respect: the same man has become both her son and her husband; and the same woman has become both his wife and his mother!

The *Psalms of Solomon*, like Paul, use the norms of the "Gentiles" to indict the people of God (cf. also Ezekiel 16:27), notably decrying both sexual immorality and impurity:

Psalms of Solomon 8:7–14[105]
I considered the judgements of God
from the creation of heaven and earth.
I justified God in his judgements,
those from the beginning of the age.
God revealed their sins
before the sun.
All the earth acknowledged the just judgements of God.
Their law-breakings were hidden in secret,
provoking wrath.
Son with mother, and father with daughter were mixed together.
Each was committing adultery with the wife of his neighbour.
They made agreements among themselves, under oath, concerning these things.

They swindled the holy places of God,
as though there were no redeeming heir.
They trampled the altar of the Lord
from all impurity
and with menstrual blood they defiled the sacrifices
as though they were common meat.
There was no sin left remaining
which they did not do beyond the Gentiles.
Because of this God mixed for them a spirit of wandering;
He gave them to drink unmixed wine, until drunk.

---

[104] The context is an argument for the excellence of Israel's laws.

[105] This Psalm reflects on the oppression that has come upon Jerusalem, and seeks to show that God is justified for having allowed it to happen.

Roman law (the *lex Julia*, put into place by Augustus) forbade the marriage of a man to his father's wife (cf. Gaius, *Institutes*, 1.63; Cicero, *Pro Cluentio*, 5.27).

And you are puffed up

It is possible that, if the man at fault here is a rich benefactor, the resistance of the church to condemning his open sin represents conventional goodwill in response to continued patronage.[106] The following Hellenistic statue base from Smyrna is illustrative of such an obligation of positive regard:

> *Inscription: Statue base from Smyrna (Hellenistic period)*
> The people
> honour Dionysius, son of Dionysius
> who is a good man on behalf of
> the citizens,
> and a benefactor of the people.

The following inscription illustrates the way in which a whole city could honour a patron (here it appears to be the father of the emperor Tiberius):

> *Inscription: Epidauros, near Corinth (13–8 BCE)*
> The city of the Epidaurions,
> For Tiberius Claudius Nero
> Their highest patron.

5:2 But shouldn't you rather be grieving, in order that the one who has done this work might be removed from your midst? 3 I for one, being absent in body but present in spirit, have already cast judgement – as though present – on the one who has done this, 4 in the name of the Lord Jesus. When you are gathered together and my spirit is with you by the power of our Lord Jesus, 5 hand this one over to Satan for the destruction of the flesh, in order that his spirit might be saved on the day of the Lord.

Hand this one over to Satan

It is possible that Deuteronomy 22:30 and 27:20 are influential for Paul here: These passages strongly condemn the marriage of a son with his father's wife (cf. Jubilees 33:10–13).

---

[106] See the discussion in chapter 6 of Clarke, *Secular Leadership*. See also John K. Chow, *Patronage and Power: A Study of Social Networks in Corinth* (Sheffield, JSOT Press, 1992); especially 139.

5:6 Your boasting is not good. Do you not know that a little yeast leavens the whole dough? 7 Clean out [καθάρατε] the old yeast, in order that you might be new dough, as in fact you are unleavened. For our Passover lamb, Christ, has been sacrificed. 8 So let us celebrate the festival, not with the old yeast – not with the yeast of evil and wickedness, but in unleavened sincerity and truth.

Clean out the old yeast

The association of "unleavened bread" and the Passover lamb arises from Exodus 12. The celebration of the Passover in a "cleansed" temple occurs in 2 Chronicles 29–30.

Early Jewish and Christian writings at times apply the image of "impurity"/"cleansing" (which are *ritual* terms) to *moral* issues that affect both individual and community:[107]

> *Philo: The Special Laws, 3.208–209*[108]
> And it must be, the lawgiver says, that everything else that the unclean person touches also becomes unclean, being defiled by its participation in that which is unclean.... For it is the unjust and ungodly person who is most properly to be thought of as unclean.
>
> *Psalms of Solomon 2:12–13*[109]
> In broad daylight they displayed
> their evil deeds.
> And the daughters of Jerusalem are polluted according to your judgement.
> For they defiled themselves in promiscuous disorder.
>
> *Testament of Reuben: 1.5–6*[110]
> Listen, my brothers, heed Reuben your father, as much as I command you: And look, I call as a witness to you today the God of heaven, that you do not go to the ignorance of youth and sexual immorality, in which I poured myself, defiling the bed of my father Jacob.

---

[107] See Jonathan Klawans, *Impurity and Sin in Ancient Judaism* (Oxford, Oxford University Press, 2000). For an alternative view see L. William Countryman, *Dirt, Greed, & Sex: Sexual Ethics in the New Testament and Their Implications for Today*, Revised Edition (Minneapolis, Fortress Press, 2007).

[108] This comes at the end of an extended section about purity laws.

[109] This psalm depicts the sins of Jerusalem that invited God's judgement.

[110] This theme, of warning about the sins of the patriarch, is a feature of the twelve Testaments.

In chapter 6, Paul will make a similar point from a positive perspective: One's body is a temple of the Holy Spirit and so should not be defiled by sexual immorality.

Philo sees yeast as representative of being "puffed up" before God:

> *Philo: The Special Laws, 1.293*[111]
> Yeast is forbidden because of the rising that comes from it. Again, this can be taken symbolically: That no one, approaching the altar, should be raised up or puffed up with arrogance.

**5:9 I wrote to you in the letter that you should not mix with the sexually immoral
– 10 not at all meaning the sexually immoral of this world, or those who are greedy and swindlers, or idolaters, in which case you would have to depart
from the world! 11 But now I am writing to you that you should not mix with anyone who is named a brother or sister, and who is sexually immoral or greedy or an idolater or a reviler or a drunkard or a swindler: with such a person, do not even eat together.
12 For what is it to me to judge those outside? Are
you not to judge those inside? 13 God will judge those outside. "Drive out the wicked one from among you."**

I wrote to you in the letter
It seems that Paul kept a record of what he had previously written. It was normal to have a professional letter-writer or secretary write up the letter to be sent as well as a copy for the sender to keep.

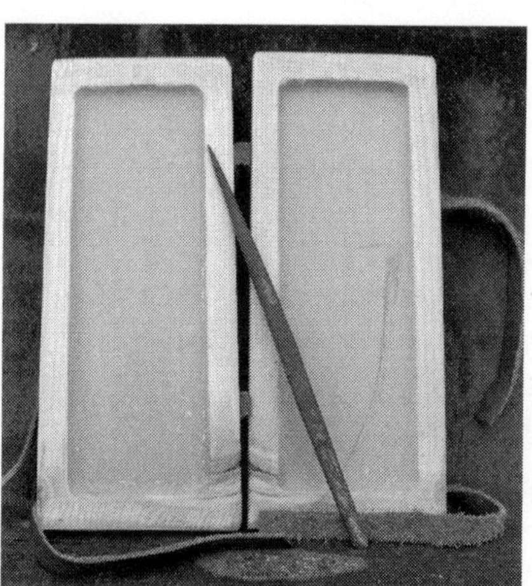

During the first century it became popular to keep personal notes on wax tablets that were inscribed with a stylus and bound together, and it may be that Paul kept information in this way.[112]

You should not mix

The imperative to be a pure, "purged" people is an important theme of Deuteronomy, occurring in chapters 13, 17, 19, 21 and 22.

---

[111] Philo is giving a symbolic interpretation of the elements of offerings.
[112] On this topic see Richards, *Paul and First Century Letter-Writing*.

Greedy or an idolater
Vice lists were common in Greco-Roman and Jewish literature. Perhaps the most extensive is found in Philo's *The Sacrifices of Abel and Cain* 32, were he lists about 150 traits of the "pleasure lover". See in the New Testament, for example, Mark 7:21–23 and Romans 1:21–32.

It may be the mention of the *greedy* here alongside the sexual immoral that leads in to the subsequent section concerning those who treat one another unjustly at court. As elsewhere in Pauline and other literature, greed and idolatry appear close together (cf. Ephesians 5:5; Colossians 3:5):

> *Testament of Judah: 19*[113]
> My children, the love of money leads to idols, because in going astray through money, people call upon those that are not gods; and the one who has it is made to fall into madness.

Drive out the wicked one from among you.
This is almost an exact quote from the repeated phrase in *Deuteronomy*, in the *Septuagint* (e.g. 17:7).[114]

6:1 If any of you has a matter against another, do you dare to take it to be judged
before the unrighteous, and not before the saints? 2 Or do you not know that
the saints will judge the world? And if the world will be judged by you, are
you unworthy to judge lesser things? 3 Do you not know that we will judge
angels – to say nothing of day to day matters?

If any of you has a matter against another
It seems that in between the two vice lists of 5:9–13 and 6:9–11, Paul departs from the discussion of sexual immorality, taking up the theme of greed. The use of "digression" or "interlude" (παρέκβασις) in Greco-Roman rhetoric is well attested, allowing the amplification or illustration of a point under consideration.

In this instance, sexual immorality and greed are juxtaposed: Sexual immorality – greed – sexual immorality. There are similar instances of rhetorical interlude in chapters 8–10 (idol meat – rights – idol meat), chapter 11 (tradition – lack of praise – tradition), and chapters 12–14 (gifts – love – gifts).

---

113 The "love of money" and "sexual immorality" are the two main themes of this Testament.

114 See the discussion of this parallel in Brian S. Rosner, *Paul, Scripture and Ethics: A Study of 1 Corinthians 5–7* (Leiden, Brill, 1994), chapter 3.

Do you not know that we will judge angels?
The idea that the people of God will join in God's future judgement is not unique to Paul. Besides Daniel 7:22; Sirach 4:15; 1 Enoch 1:9; 10:11–14, 67–8; 91:15; and 1QpHab 5:4, see:

> *Wisdom of Solomon 3:8*[115]
> They will judge the nations, and rule over peoples, and the Lord will rule over them for eternity.

> *Testament of Abraham: Recension A, Chapter 13, lines 18–20*[116]
> And at the second coming, all breath and all creation will be judged by the twelve tribes of Israel.

The judgement of fallen angels is mentioned in Isaiah 24:21; 2 Peter 2:4 and Jude 6.

6:4 If you have lawsuits in day to day matters then, do you seek rulings from those who are scorned by the church? 5 I say this to shame you. So is there no one wise among you, who will be able to decide cases between their brothers and sisters?

Lawsuits in day to day matters
Lawsuits were very common in Roman society, and arguably favoured the rich.[117] Dio Chrysostom says of late first century Corinth:

> *Dio Chrysostom: Eighth Discourse: On Virtue (Diogenes), 8.9*[118]
> And there at this time, around the temple of Poseidon, one could hear . . . myriads of lawyers, twisting judgements.

Do you seek rulings
At the far side of the agora in the centre of this picture (opposite) is the *bema*, the "tribunal" where significant rulings were announced to the people:

---

115 This refers to the immortal souls of the once-persecuted righteous.

116 Abraham is here depicted as foreseeing God's final judgement.

117 For an exploration of this topic in relation to Corinth, see Bruce W. Winter, "Civil Litigation in Secular Corinth and the Church" *New Testament Studies* 37/04 (1991), 559–572. On the problems of legal corruption in Roman provinces, see Cicero, *Pro Caecina*, 73.

118 Dio is lamenting the superficiality of the city.

Paul himself was questioned in Corinth by proconsul Gallio, according to Acts 18:12–15.

I say this to shame you

As elsewhere in the letter, it is evident that Paul is utilising the theme of honour and shame that was so strong in Roman Corinth. For those whose intense desire was to receive acclaim, the suggestion of "shame" constituted a sharp warning. Plutarch's comments illustrate the fear of shame that was characteristic of Roman culture:

> *Plutarch: Life of Agis, 7–8*[119]
> Now these thoughts on pursuing honour with the masses came to us in considering the outworking of this pursuit in the adversities of Tiberius and Gaius of Granchus. Having received the best nature, the best upbringing, and the best political policies, they were destroyed not so much by the unrestrained desire for glory, as by the fear of disgrace – arising from motives that were not, to begin with, sordid. For they had been greatly obliged to the people for their goodwill, so that they were ashamed to fail to repay the debt. Rather, they attempted to outdo the honours given to them, with kind services.

Is there no one wise among you?
Paul's ironic question to those who yearn for wisdom reveals that they ought to be ashamed to bring petty matters before public courts. The Society of Iobacchi in the second century similarly held that internal strife must be judged by insiders rather than outsiders:

> *Inscription: Athens (178 CE) Lines 90–94*[120]
> And let the same punishment come upon the one who is struck and yet does not bring the case before the priest or the chief-Bacchus, but rather brings charges before public courts.

---

[119] This is presented as a warning of the dangers of ambitiously chasing public applause.

[120] This inscription outlines the expectations for members of this association, including requirements for membership, payment, conduct, and worship.

In Exodus 18:13–26 and Deuteronomy 1:9–17, Moses is depicted as appointing elders to judge disputes among the people of Israel. It may be that Paul's expectations for believers arise from Judaism's inheritance of this tradition.[121]

6:6 But brother brings judgement against brother, and this in front of unbelievers! 7 Already it is really a defeat for you that you have lawsuits with one another. Why not rather be treated unjustly? Why not rather be robbed? 8 But instead you treat unjustly and rob, and you do this to brothers and sisters!

Why not rather be treated unjustly?
Musonius Rufus urges that philosophers, as sensible people, should accept personal injury rather than bring it to court:

> *Musonius Rufus: Will the Philosopher Prosecute Anyone for Personal Injury? (Discourse 10)*[122]
> For in what way does the one who suffers do wrong? It is the one who does wrong who is immediately disgraced, while the one who suffers – as one who does no wrong in suffering – comes to no disgrace. Therefore the person who has sense would not go to court or bring charges.

6:9 Or do you not know that the unrighteous will not inherit the kingdom of God? Do not be deceived: neither the sexually immoral nor idolaters nor adulterers nor the sexually perverse nor homosexual offenders 10 nor thieves nor the greedy nor drunkards nor revilers nor swindlers will inherit the kingdom of God. 11 And some of you were these things. But you were washed; but you were sanctified; but you were justified in the name of our Lord Jesus Christ and in the Spirit of our God.

12 "Everything is lawful for me" – but not everything is beneficial. "Everything is lawful for me" – but I will not come under the authority of anything. 13 "Food is for the belly, and the belly for food, and God will bring an end to both one and the other."

"Everything is lawful for me"
The nature and limits of personal freedom were topics discussed by Greco-Roman philosophers and writers, who reached various conclusions. Epictetus and Dio Chrysostom are illustrative:

---

122 See the discussion in Rosner, *Paul, Scripture and Ethics*, chapter 4.

123 This discourse urges philosophers not to return evil for evil, but to accept petty suffering.

Epictetus: Discourses: Concerning Freedom, 4.1.1[123]
The free person is the one who lives as they please, for whom there is neither necessity nor hindrance nor constraint; whose pursuits are unimpeded, whose desires are attained, whose weaknesses are avoided.

4.1.151
"You then," someone says, "are you free?" I wish to the gods and pray to be so, but yet I am unable to look my masters in the face; I still value that which is bodily, doing much to perfect it, although I do not have it perfectly.

Dio Chrysostom: Fourteenth Discourse: On Slavery and Freedom, 14.13[124]
"But surely we may put this matter into one word: That for whomever it is lawful to do what one desires, that person is free; but for whomever it is not lawful, that person is a slave."

No; not concerning the person on a ship, or the sick, or soldiers, or those learning to write or to play the kithara or to wrestle or to do any other art can you say this! For it is not lawful for these to do as they want, but rather to do what the captain or doctor or teacher instructs. Neither therefore is it lawful for the others to do as they please; but if anyone should act against the orders that have been put in place, they will be punished.

6:13 But the body is not for sexual immorality, but for the Lord – and the Lord
for the body. 14 And God also raised the Lord, and will raise us through his
power. 15 Do you not know that your bodies are parts of Christ? Shall I then
make a part of Christ a part of a prostitute? May it not be! 16 Do you not know
that the one who unites himself to a prostitute is one flesh with her? For it
says:

The two of them will become one flesh.

17 But the one who is united to the Lord is one spirit with him. 18 Flee from
sexual immorality! "Every sin that a person does is external to the body." But
the one who commits sexual immorality sins against their own body. 19 Or do
you not know that your body is a temple of the Holy Spirit who is in you,
whom you have from God, and you are not your own? 20 For you were bought
at great cost. Therefore glorify God in your body.

---

[123] This is the beginning of Book 4, setting out an opening premise.

[124] The opening quotation comes from the mouth of an interlocutor, who assumes too quickly that freedom involves unfettered desire.

The body is not meant for sexual immorality but for the Lord – and the Lord for the body

The human body was celebrated in Greco-Roman sculpture and artwork;[125] but even in the more overtly sexual Greek era, the noble enjoyment of bodily beauty was related to an appreciation of the beauty of the soul. Uncontrolled lust was frowned upon and ridiculed in art (as can be seen in the presentation of the god Pan).

Demosthenes: Erotic Essay, 61.6[126]

Therefore I have been all the more moved to write this message, not wanting to miss out on directing toward two goods. For, beginning to describe to you your good qualities, I hope at the same time to demonstrate both that you are desirable, and that, being thus, I am not senseless if I love you. And in offering this most pressing advice, I will show my own goodwill and provide a basis for our common friendship.

---

[125] The term "Greco-Roman" is fitting here, as one often comes across Roman copies of previously existing Greek sculptures.

[126] This is a letter to a young man, urging him to make the most of his youthful beauty of body and soul.

61.8

All will agree with me that for those of such an age as yours it is most pressing to have beauty of appearance, and prudence of soul, and manliness with regard to both of these, and consistently to have gracefulness of speech.

Aphrodite, whose temple had been the greatest of Corinth's Greek era, and who remained important in the Roman era, was able to represent both "heavenly" love and purity, as well as – paradoxically – an object of earthly desire (cf. Plato's *Symposium*). She is depicted in the third picture from the left as rejecting the lustful advances of Pan. The statue of Aphrodite in the middle of the lower picture is from Ancient Corinth:

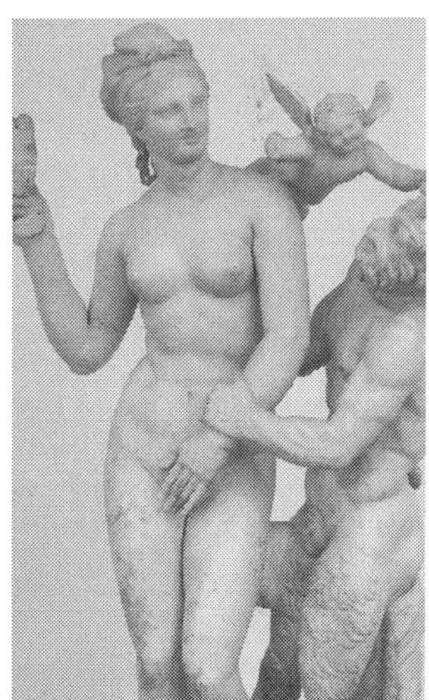

Roman moralists praised self-control and sexual morality, condemning and ridiculing men who were perceived as (openly) licentious or effeminate.[127] Seneca condemns the drunkenness and sexual indulgence that were possible for a licentious slave owner (cf. Philo, *The Contemplative Life*, 50–52):

> *Seneca: Epistles, 47.7*[128]
> Another slave, the wine server, must wrestle back his age to model feminine attire. He is not able to escape boyhood, but is called back to it. And though he has the body of a soldier, his face is kept smooth, and body hair plucked out from the roots. And he is kept on watch all night, divided between his lord's drunkenness and lust. And in the bedroom he is a man, but at the banquet, he is a boy.

Attitudes to sex and the body in Roman Corinth, then, existed within a complex society and history that included a variety of perspectives such as admiration for the body, dismissal of the body, the disdain of public licentiousness, and opportunities for private indulgence.

Do you not know that your bodies are members of Christ?
Epictetus calls his hearers to act as though they carry God around in their bodies, affecting him with all of their actions (cf. Seneca, *Epistles* 41.1–2):

> *Epictetus: Discourses, 2.8.11–16*[129]
> But you are superior [to plants and animals]. You are a piece of God. You have in yourself a part of him. Why then are you ignorant of your relationality? Why do you not know where you came from? Do you not want to recall, when you eat, who you are as the eater, and to whom you are giving food? Or when you combine in intercourse, who it is that combines? When you are in company, when you exercise, when you discuss: do you not know that it is God you are feeding, God you are exercising? You are carrying around God, fool, and you are ignorant of it! Do you think I am talking about a god of gold or silver, who is external? You carry him within yourself, blemishing him without perceiving it with your unclean thoughts and dirty actions!

---

[127] See chapter 2 of Alistair Scott May, *"The Body for the Lord": Sex and Identity in 1 Corinthians 5–7* (London, T&T Clark, 2004).

[128] In this letter Seneca is bemoaning the way that slaves are degraded by their masters.

[129] The context is a discussion of the nature of the "good", and its relation to God.

The two of you will become one flesh
This is a quotation of Genesis 2:24, following the Septuagint.

The one who unites himself to a prostitute
There were different types of commercial sex workers in the Greco-Roman world. *Hetairas* might live at the expense of a particular rich man for an indefinite period of time, or might regularly entertain at banquets. Prostitutes might host clients at their own dwellings, or seek clients at the agora or elsewhere in public.

The warning of Sirach 19:2 bears some similarity to Paul's argument here:

> *Sirach 19:2*[130]
> Wine and women lead those with understanding astray, and the one who unites with prostitutes is reckless. Decay and worms will be such a person's inheritance, and the reckless soul will be expelled. Those who entrust themselves to others hastily have shallow hearts, and those who sin will upset their own soul.

The one who is united to the Lord is one spirit with him
Perhaps Paul is drawing upon the Old Testament image of the marital union between the Lord and Israel (e.g. Ezekiel 16; Hosea 3).

Flee from sexual immorality
The *Testament of Reuben* uses exactly the same phrase in 5:5. It may be that both the *Testament* and Paul are drawing on the imagery of Joseph, who fled from Potiphar's wife in Genesis 39.[131]

You were bought at great cost. Therefore glorify God in your body.
The slave's body was thought of as the master's possession, as illustrated in Aristophanes' play ***Plutus***:

> *Aristophanes: Plutus, Lines 1–7*[132]
> Cario [a slave]:
> How painful a thing it is, O Zeus and the gods,
> to be the slave of a foolish master.

---

[130] This occurs within a section that urges self-control.

[131] See Brian S. Rosner, "A Possible Quotation of Test. Reuben 5:5 in 1 Corinthians 6:18a", *Journal of Theological Studies* 43/1 (1992), 123–7.

[132] Cario is complaining, because his master has decided to become a follower of a blind man.

For he may give the best of advice,
but if the master does not do what has been advised,
it is necessary for the slave to share the burden of his evils.
For the gods have not permitted the exerciser of the body to control his body,
but rather the one who has bought it.

The language of "buying" also has significance in the New Testament, as the concept of God's "redemption" of Israel from slavery in Egypt (e.g. Exodus 6:6) is seen as foreshadowing God's greater work of redemption in Jesus (e.g. Galatians 3:13–14).

7:1 Now concerning the things about which you wrote: "It is good for a man not to touch his wife". 2 But because of the problems of sexual immorality, let each of you have sex with your own wife, or your own husband. 3 The husband ought to give himself to his wife, and likewise also the wife to her husband. 4 The wife does not exercise authority over her own body, but the husband does. And likewise, the husband does not exercise authority over his own body, but the wife does. 5 Do not rob one another, except perhaps by agreement for a period, in order that you might devote yourselves to prayer; and then come together again, in order that you might not be tempted by Satan because of your lack of self-control. 6 But I say this as a concession, and not as a command. 7 But I wish that all people could be as I myself am. But each has their own gift from God: one has this, the other has that.

"It is good for a man not to touch his wife"[133]

The topic of sexual purity was the source of some debate among Greco-Roman thinkers and writers. One prominent (especially Stoic) view was that, in order to preserve the purpose or nobility of the marriage relationship, sexual *pleasure* should not be sought in the marriage bed. This may provide a background to the Corinthian slogan that Paul is countering:[134]

Musonius Rufus: Concerning Sexual Indulgence (Discourse 12)[135]

Not the least part of the life of luxury is also sexual passion, because those

133 That the wording refers to sexual pleasure is confirmed by Roy E. Ciampa, "Revisiting the Euphemism in 1 Corinthians 7.1" in *Journal for the Study of the New Testament* 31/3 (2009), 325–338.

134 See Deming, *Paul on Marriage and Celibacy.*

135 Musonius' comments about marriage exhibit a standard Stoic insistence that those who marry are obligated to raise children.

who live this luxurious life feel needful of a variety of lovers, not only lawful but also unlawful, neither only women but also men; hunting one or another lover, and not being satisfied with those that are at hand, they send for those that are more rare, and seek shameful types of intercourse, all of which are a great charge against humanity. Those who are not luxurious or evil consider sexual passion only to be justified when it is in marriage, and then should only be carried out for the begetting of children, because this is lawful – but when pursued for mere pleasure it is unjust and unlawful, even in marriage. But of all sorts of intercourse it is the adulterous that are most unlawful, and of these, none is more immoderate than that of men with men, because such a reckless thing is against nature.

Ocellus Lucanas: On the Nature of the Universe, 44[136]
First, then, this must be understood: We come together not for the sake of pleasure but for the generation of children. For also, sexual abilities themselves, and the organs, and the desires for intercourse given by God to humans, do not happen to have been given for the sake of pleasure, but for the eternal continuation of the race.

Antipater of Tarsus: On Marriage, Lines 13 – 15[137]
Aiming, both while living and after having passed away, to defend and aid the fatherland, they [i.e. good citizens] think of uniting in marriage as among their necessities and foremost duties, being eager to fulfil all that nature puts on them.

Plutarch: Advice to Bride and Groom, 140/16[138]
If then a man, who in private is uncontrolled and dissolute with regard to pleasures, should commit a misdeed with a *hetaira* or a female servant, his wife ought not to be irritated or angry, reasoning that his drunken debauchery and licentiousness and lust have been shared with another, out of regard for her.

---

136 This is part of an argument that sex ought to be used to produce good offspring, something that will only come about through morally pure intercourse.

137 This is part of an argument that the noble young man ought to pursue marriage for the sake of the increase of the fatherland and the bolstering that comes from partnership.

138 Plutarch is giving guidance about what will be considered virtuous for the newly married couple. See also Quintilian, *Institutes of Oratory*, 6.2.14, where Quintilian commends restraint towards one's wife, as evidence of genuine affection.

142/29
So a husband should reason about his virtuous and austere wife, "I am not able to have the same woman as both wife and *hetaira*."

Testament of Naphtali 8:8[139]
For there is a time for intercourse with a man's wife, and a time for self-control in order that he might pray.

There may also be precedent for this sort of view in Jewish literature. Tobit 4:12–13 hints that the desire for a Gentile wife may spring "from every kind of sexual immorality" (πάσης πορνείας), indicating that such lust is unacceptable in marriage:

Tobit 4:12–13
Guard yourself, child, from every kind of sexual immorality, and first of all take a wife from the seed of your fathers. Do not take a foreign wife, a woman who is not from your father's tribe – because we are sons of the prophets. Remember, child, Noah, Abraham, Isaac, Jacob – our ancestors from ancient times – these all took wives from their families, and they were blessed in their children, and their seed will inherit the earth.

The husband ought to give himself to his wife
Exodus 21:10 commands husbands not to withhold food, clothing and marital rights from a neglected wife.

7:8 Now I say to those who are unmarried, and to widows: It is good for them if they can remain as I am; 9 but if they are not able to control themselves, let them marry, for it is better to marry than to burn. 10 But to those who are married, I command – not I, but the Lord – that a wife should not be separated from her husband; 11 but if she is, let her remain unmarried or be reconciled to her husband. And a husband should not leave his wife.

Not I, but the Lord
It is only in 1 Corinthians and 1 Thessalonians (e.g. 4:15) that Paul quotes sayings "from the Lord". It may be that Paul is here drawing on the saying later recorded in Mark 10:11–12.

Better to marry than to burn
Sirach also utilises the image of burning for sexual desire:

139 This *Testament* is especially concerned that things be done in their proper order.

> *Sirach 23:16 (Septuagint 23:16–17)*[140]
> Two sights multiply sins, and a third brings on wrath. A soul, burning as hot as fire, will not be quenched until it burns out. A man who is sexually immoral in his body of flesh will not cease until he is burnt by fire. To a sexually immoral man, all bread is sweet. He will never grow weary until he dies.

Similarly to Paul, Epictetus grants a concession to those who are distracted by love, in *Discourses*, 3.22.76.

A woman should not be separated from her husband
Roman law and custom made no distinction between divorce and separation. There is no reason to think that Paul intends a distinction in meaning here. Remarriage after divorce was legal and normal.[141]

A number of marriage contracts from the era survive:

> *Papyrus: GBU 1052 (13* BCE*)*
> To Protarchus from Thermion, the daughter of Apion, with her custodian Apollonius son of Chaireas, and from Apollonius son of Ptolemaeus. Thermion and Apollonius of Ptolemaeus are in agreement that they have come together to share life in common. And Apollonius of Ptolemaeus has collected by hand from Thermion, from the house, a dowry of a pair of gold earrings weighing three quarters and silver drachmas. From now on, Apollonnius of Ptolemaeus will supply to Thermion all of her needs and clothing, as his wedded wife – according to the ability of his means. And he will not treat her badly or throw her out or insult her or take on another wife. Or else, if he does these things, he will immediately make full repayment of the dowry, plus half – coming from Apollonius of Ptolemaeus himself, as well as his property, by legal process. And Thermion will act rightly toward her husband and their common life, and will not sleep away from him or stay away from the house by day without the permission of Apollonius of Ptolemaeus. And she will not ruin or damage their common home, or go to another man. Or else, if she is proven to have done these things, she will have the dowry taken away and will suffer the appropriate fine. Seventeenth year of Caesar, Pharmouthi 20.

---

140 This chapter is devoted to sins of the tongue (7–15) and sins of desire (16–27).

141 See David Instone-Brewer, "1 Corinthians 7 in the Light of the Graeco-Roman Marriage and Divorce Papyri" *Tyndale Bulletin* 52/1 (2001), 101–116; "1 Corinthians 7 in the Light of the Jewish Greek and Aramaic Marriage and Divorce Papyri", *Tyndale Bulletin* 52/2 (2001), 225–243.

> *Rylands papyrus 154 (66 CE)*
> If a difference comes between them and they are separated from one another – whether Thaisarion is sent away by Chaeremon or she voluntarily leaves him – the property in question will belong to Thaisarion's father Sisois. Or if he is no longer alive, the inheritance of ten and three-quarter arurae will belong to Thaisarion herself.

Josephus explains the Jewish custom – that a husband, but not a wife, may initiate divorce – in *Antiquities*, 15.259.

7:12 To the rest, I say – I, not the Lord – that if any brother has an unbelieving wife, and she is happy to live with him, he should not leave her. 13 And if any woman has an unbelieving husband, and he is happy to live with her, she should not leave him. 14 For the unbelieving husband is made holy by the wife. And the unbelieving wife is made holy by the believing brother. Otherwise your children would be unclean, but as it is they are holy. 15 But if the unbeliever separates, let them separate. The brother or sister in these circumstances is not bound. God has called you to peace. 16 How do you know, wife, whether you will save your husband? How do you know, husband, whether you will save your wife?

Otherwise your children would be unclean, but as it is they are holy
Pseudo-Phocylides indicates that children might be considered "unclean" if they are not from a legitimate marriage:

> *Pseudo-Phocylides: Sentences, 177–178*[142]
> Do not prostitute your spouse, defiling your children,
> for the adulterous bed does not produce children in your likeness.

It may be, alternatively, that their present "holiness" arises from the ethical influence of the believing family members.

7:17 Otherwise, each should remain as the Lord has apportioned: Each should continue to walk just as God has called them. And this is what I direct in all the churches. 18 If anyone was circumcised when called, let them not try to undo it. If anyone was uncircumcised when called, let them not get circumcised. 19 Circumcision is nothing and uncircumcision is nothing; what matters is keeping the commands of God. 20 Let each person remain in that calling in which they were called.

Each should remain as the Lord has apportioned
This may have sounded like a Stoic position to Paul's hearers in Corinth, apparently emphasising the need to accept one's fate. However, Paul

[142] This occurs in a section about marriage, purity, and family.

does seem to encourage slaves to pursue freedom (below; the interpretation is debated), and presents his exhortation as a liberation from constraint: One does not *need* to pursue circumcision or uncircumcision.

Let them not try to undo it
In *1 Maccabees,* "undoing circumcision" represents the repudiation of Judaism because of a willingness to give in to Gentile rulers:

> *1 Maccabees: 1:15*[143]
> And they made themselves uncircumcised, and departed from the holy covenant, and joined themselves to the Gentiles, and were sold into doing evil.

Josephus elucidates:

> *Josephus: Jewish Antiquities, 12.241*[144]
> So they appealed to him [Antiochus] to give them permission to build a gymnasium in Jerusalem. And having received this permission, they also concealed the circumcision of their private parts, so as to be Greeks even when undressed.

An operation for reversing circumcision is described in the first century work *De Medicina*, 7.25, by Aulus Cornelius Celsus.

7:21 If you were a slave when called, do not let it trouble you; but if you are able to become free, take the opportunity. 22 For the one called as a slave in the Lord is the Lord's freed person, and likewise the one called as a free person is Christ's slave. 23 You were bought at great cost; do not become slaves of humans. 24 Brothers and sisters, let each person remain, before God, in the situation in which they were called.

If you were a slave
Status and lifestyle in Roman Corinth were somewhat complex.[145] Being a slave meant having a low rank; but depending on the master and responsibilities, it was not always a dreadful existence.

---

143 This disparagingly refers to those who pursued the Hellenisation associated with Antiochus Epiphanes.

144 Josephus is also describing the events associated with the Jews who pursued Hellenisation at the time of Antiochus Epiphanes. See also Philo, *Special Laws* 1.2.

145 On the topic of slavery in relation to Paul's writings, see S. Scott Bartchy, *First-Century Slavery and 1 Corinthians 7:21* (Society of Biblical Literature, 1973); and Dale B. Martin, *Slavery as Salvation: The Metaphor of Slavery in Pauline Christianity* (New Haven and London, Yale University Press, 1990).

Florentinus: Institutes 9 (Digesta Iustiniani I.5.4)[146]
Freedom is the natural faculty to do that which one chooses to do, except that which is prohibited by force or by law. Slavery is instituted by the *law of nations*, according to which a person is subjected, contrary to nature, to the ownership of another person.

Aeschylus' poetic observation, while from a different era, remains illustrative of the variety of experiences of slavery through to the Roman period:

Aeschylus: Agamemnon, 1039–1045[147]
Clytaemestra:
Do not be over-proud,
For it is said that even the son of Alceme once
Tolerated being sold, eating the food of slavery.
But if such a thing as this must, of necessity, be one's fate,
One should be thankful to belong to masters who have *inherited* their riches.
For those who have reaped more riches than was expected of them
Act in all severity toward their slaves, crossing the line.

In first century Greece, most people entered slavery not through war but through birth (by being born to a mother who was a slave); through crime (as a punishment); through debt (as a payment); or by selling themselves for a certain period (cf. Philo, *Every Good Man is Free*, 35–7).

Dio Chrysostom: On Slavery and Freedom 15.14[148]
What then: Did not many Athenians of those captured in Sicily enslave themselves in Sicily and in the Peloponnese even though they were free? And in many other battles there were some who enslaved themselves for a time until they found people who would release them; and others enslaved themselves until the end!

Oxyrhynchus papyrus 722 (91 or 107 CE)
I, Achilleus, together with my brother Sarapas, have freed the third part of the slave Apollonous, and I have received the ransom of two hundred silver drachmas.

---

[146] This is a digest of Roman laws, edited together in the 6th century.

[147] Cassandra is being urged not to look down on being in the service of Zeus.

[148] Dio is telling the story of a conversation overheard between a free man and a slave. The free man boasts of his freedom, and the slave points out that the line between freedom and slavery is not always clear.

Epictetus observes that slaves generally desired freedom – even though they may have had an unrealistic picture of fending for oneself:

> *Epictetus: Discourses 4.1.32–33*[149]
> The slave wishes to be set free immediately. Why? Do you think the slave wants to give money to the tax collectors? No; but they want to be set free because they imagine that until now, because they have not experienced it, they have been constrained and unlucky.

Seneca urges that slaves should be thought of as real people, and that noble masters should relate to them on friendly terms.

> *Seneca: Epistles, 47.1*[150]
> I am made pleased, by those who come from you, to find out that you are on friendly terms with those who live as your slaves. This is fitting for a wise and educated man such as yourself. "They are slaves!" On the contrary; they are humans. "They are slaves!" On the contrary; they are comrades. "They are slaves!" On the contrary; they are lowly friends. "They are slaves!" On the contrary; they are fellow-slaves, if one considers that we are equally owned by fortune.

The one called as a slave in the Lord is the Lord's freed person
In his work *Every Good Man is Free*, Philo develops the argument that everyone who primarily desires virtue can never truly be constrained:

> *Philo: Every Good Man is Free, 60*[151]
> Thus the virtuous person cannot be a slave.

7:25 Now concerning virgins I do not have a command from the Lord; but I give you my opinion as one who, by the Lord's mercy, is faithful: 26 I think that it is good for people to remain as they are, because of this present crisis [ἀνάγκης]. 27 If you are promised to a wife, do not seek to be released. If you have been released from a wife, do not seek a wife. 28 But if you marry, you have not sinned; and if the virgin marries, she has not sinned. But these will have suffering in the flesh; and I would spare you from this.

---

149 Epictetus' broader point is that the slave may in fact fall into a greater "slavery" when free.

150 Seneca goes on to lament the loss of the time when masters and slaves used to eat and converse together, and when consequently slaves loved their masters, rather than resenting them.

151 Philo's point in context is that only the wise person is truly free.

This present crisis

Paul may be interpreting present events (perhaps the grain shortage that had hit the area by the time of Paul's letter – see Tacitus, *Annals* 12.43.1; Suetonius, *Claudius*, 18.2) in the light of Old Testament characterisations of crisis (e.g. Jeremiah 16:2; cf. Ezekiel 7:12; Daniel 12:1; 6 Ezra 16:40–44). Alternatively, the "present crisis" may be the "problems of sexual immorality" mentioned in 7:2.

The apocalyptic *Book of the Watchers* begins by depicting a climactic "day of crisis":

> *1 Enoch 1:1*[152]
> The message of blessing from Enoch, with which he blessed the righteous elect who were to come in the day of crisis [ἀνάγκης], when all the enemies would rise up – and the righteous would be saved.

7:29 What I am saying, brothers and sisters, is this: the time has been shortened. From now on, those who have wives should live as though they do not; 30 and those who mourn should live as though they do not; and those who buy as though they did not hold onto their purchases; 31 and those who deal with the world as though they did not, for the form of this world is passing away. 32 And I want you to be free of cares.

I want you to be free of cares

Epictetus considers that the Cynic ought to be devoted to the service of God, rather than tied down by human commitments:

> *Epictetus: Discourses, 3.22.47–8*[153]
> Look at me: I am without a house, without a city, without property, without slaves. I sleep on the ground. I have no wife, no children, no praetorium, but only the earth and the sky and one cloak. And what do I need? Am I not free of pain? Am I not free of fear? Am I not free?

However, unlike Epictetus, the basis for Paul's directives is that the "time has been shortened".

---

[152] This introductory verse situates the *Book of the Watchers* as an apocalyptic exhortation from righteous Enoch.

[153] In this discourse, Epictetus sees Cynics as devoting themselves fully to their cause, refusing to be distracted by lesser concerns than the need to impart wisdom. This Cynic vision of marriage is clearly at odds with the Stoic idea that procreative marriage can be a godly pursuit of ordered harmony.

Philo describes the rejection of marriage by the Essenes in similar terms:

> *Philo: Hypothetica, 2.17*[154]
> For the man who is captured by the love charms of his wife, or who, because of the impulse of nature, cares for his children, is no longer the same toward the others, but has become a different person, no longer free but a slave.

7:32 The one who is not married cares about the things of the Lord – how to
please the Lord. 33 But the man who is married cares about the things of the
world – how to please his wife, 34 and he is divided. And the unmarried woman and the virgin care about the things of the Lord – that they might be holy both in body and in spirit. But the woman who is married cares about the things of
the world – how to please her husband. 35 I am saying this for your benefit, not in order to put a noose on you, but for your fitting and undivided devotion to the Lord.

How to please the Lord
Antipater of Tarsus expresses a Stoic view of marriage as a relationship that aims to please the husband, before the wife:

> *Antipater of Tarsus: On Marriage, Lines 25–29*[155]
> But also in another way [the marriage partnership] is, in all probability, the greatest: For other partnerships also have different sorts of diversions; "but these [that is, marriages] necessarily look to one soul", which is that of the husband. For she gives herself, while father and mother are healthy and not intellectually incapable, to make this her one vision in life, and her goal: to please him.

7:36 But if any man thinks that he is acting in an unfitting way toward his engaged virgin – if he is beyond restraint, and thus compelled, let him act on
his wishes. He is not sinning; let him marry. 37 But whoever stands firm in his own heart, without compulsion but having control over his own will, having
decided in his own heart to keep her as a virgin, he will do well. 38 So the one who causes his engaged virgin to marry does well, and the one who does not cause his engaged virgin to marry will do better.

---

[154] This comes at the end of a glowing description of the Essenes. Sections 14–17 concern their attitudes toward women and marriage.

[155] Antipater goes on to say that after the husband's parents die, he is to devote himself to his wife.

His engaged virgin
Pseudo-Phocylides calls for virgins to be hidden from view, and their beauty guarded (cf. Sirach 42:9–14):

> *Pseudo-Phocylides: Sentences, 215–17*[156]
> And guard a virgin in well-locked inner rooms,
> and do not let her be seen in front of the house before her wedding day.

In Achilles Tatius' romantic fiction, Clitophon insists that he has "kept" his beloved Leucippe a virgin (through a time of crisis) until they can marry:

> *Achilles Tatius: The Adventures of Leucippe and Clitophon, 8.18*[157]
> For I have kept the young woman as a virgin right up until now!

The one who does not cause his engaged virgin to marry will do better
Epictetus specifically urges that Cynics should not distract themselves with marriage, given the upheaval of the times (cf. Pseudo-Diogenes, *Epistle* 47):

> *Epictetus: Discourses, 3.22.76*[158]
> We are enquiring into common marriages and those free of distractions, and in this enquiry we have found that in the current state of affairs, this act is not best for the Cynic.

7:39 A wife is bound to her husband for as long as he lives. But if the husband should die, she is free to be married to whomever she wishes, but only in the Lord. 40 But she is more blessed if she remains as she is, in my opinion. And I think I also have the Spirit of God.

But only in the Lord
The phrase "in the Lord" occurs at a number of important points in 1 Corinthians (1:31; 4:17; 9:1–2; 11:11; 15:58), reminding that the life of the believer is defined by their relation to Christ. The directive to marry "in the Lord" probably has its background in similar commands in the Old Testament (e.g. Deuteronomy 7:3).

---

156 In this section of the *Sentences*, Pseudo-Phocylides gives directions for respectable relationships, and urges that the beauty of both male and female children should be carefully guarded.

157 In the story, the couple prove their innocence and receive their fathers' blessing to marry.

158 Epictetus likens the present time to a period of battle.

The Cross Applied II: Discern the Body

8:1–11:1: Knowledge and Rights

8:1 Now concerning meat sacrificed to idols, we know that "we all have knowledge". Knowledge puffs up, but love builds up. 2 But if anyone thinks they know anything, they do not yet know as they ought to know. 3 But if anyone loves God, such a person is known by him. 4 Concerning food that has been sacrificed to idols, we know that no idol in the world really exists, and that there is no God but one. 5 For even if there are so-called gods, whether in heaven or on earth – as indeed there are many "gods" and many "lords" –

6 But for us there is one God, the Father; from whom are all things, and for whom we exist;

And one Lord, Jesus Christ; through whom are all things, and through whom we exist.

Food that has been sacrificed to idols

4 Maccabees depicts a situation in which Hebrews are challenged to eat meat sacrificed to idols, or face their own deaths:

> *4 Maccabees 5:1–3*[159]
>
> Sitting in a certain high place with his counsellors and armed soldiers standing around him, the tyrant Antiochus ordered the bodyguards to drag over each one of the Hebrews, and force them to taste pork and meat sacrificed to idols. But if any of them were unwilling to eat the abominable meats, they were to be turned on the wheel of torture and killed.

159 In context, eating such food represents a repudiation of Judaism and an acceptance of foreign tyranny.

No idol in the world really exists

The command to avoid idols had been given in Exodus 20:4–5. Later, the non-reality and folly of Gentile idols had become an important motif in Jewish works. The apocryphal *Letter of Jeremiah* is illustrative (cf. Psalm 115:1–5; Jeremiah 10:1–6; Wisdom of Solomon 13:10):

> *Letter of Jeremiah: Baruch 6:3–6*[160]
> Now you will see in Babylon gods of silver and gold and wood, carried on people's shoulders, feared by the Gentiles. So do not let yourselves become like those barbaric people, or take on their fear, when you see a crowd in front of the gods and behind them, worshipping them. But say in your head, "I must worship you, O Master!"

There is one God . . . and one Lord

It is possible that Paul is adapting the *shema* here – the regularly repeated monotheistic affirmation of Deuteronomy 6:4–5. For Paul, the "one God" must now be understood in relation to the "one Lord" Jesus Christ.

Philo makes a somewhat similar statement about the world being produced from materials "by" God and "through" the word:

> *Philo: On the Cherubim, 127*[161]
> Leaving aside, then, these "partial" buildings, let us consider the greatest building or city, which is the world. For you will find that its cause is God, by whom it came to be; its material is the four elements, from which it was constructed; its instrument is the word of God, through which it was built; and the purpose of the building is the goodness of the Designer.

Seneca rehearses the views of the Stoics, Aristotle, and Plato in similar terms, viewing the "maker" as the first cause:

> *Seneca: Epistles, 65.8*[162]
> Therefore there are five causes, as Plato says: That *from* which it comes, that *by* which it comes, that *into* which it comes, that *toward* which it comes, and that *because* of which it comes.

---

[160] These introductory verses set the tone and content of the whole (chapter-long) letter.

[161] Philo's emphasis in context is that God should be thought of as *cause* rather than *instrument*.

[162] This is a letter in which Seneca asks a friend to "referee" a debate about *cause* and *matter*.

8:7 But this knowledge is not present in everyone: for some, their custom until now has been to eat idol-meat as though it were truly of an idol, and their conscience, being weak, is bruised. 8 But food does not present us to God: if we do not eat, we lack nothing; and if we do eat, we are no better off. 9 But watch out that this "right" of yours does not become a stumbling block to the weak.

This right of yours

The "right" to accept invitations to dine at civic-hosted cult meals was desirable in terms of maintaining social esteem, and perhaps involved the possibility of participating in indulgent activities. Numerous banquet invitations survive, from a slightly later period:

> *Oxyrhynchus papyri (2nd/3rd Century)*
> Nikephoros invites you to dine at a banquet of the lord Sarapis, in the Birth-House on the 23rd, from the 9th hour.
>
> Herais invites you to dine in the room of the Sarapeion for a banquet of the lord Sarapis, tomorrow, which is the 11th, from the 9th hour.
>
> The god summons you to a banquet being held in the Thoereion tomorrow from the 9th hour.

Roman Corinth had a great many temples and shrines, the most famous of which is the Temple of Apollo, below (right):

At the foot of Acrocorinth, which is pictured below, was the cult of Demeter and Persephone. It had cult-dining rooms catering for 200 people during its Greek period. These appear to have been no longer in use by the city's Roman period:

A stumbling block to the weak

Horace relates the story of a conversation with a friend. The friend, annoyingly, refuses to speak, ostensibly because he is too "weak" to want to offend Jewish sensibilities:

> *Horace: Satires 1.9.68–72*[163]
>
> "I am well aware [that there is something I have to tell you]; but I will tell you at a better time. Today is the thirtieth Sabbath. Would you want to offend the circumcised Jews?"
>
> "Decency", I reply, "is nothing to me!"
>
> "But it is to me: I am a bit weaker, one of many who are so. Excuse me – I will speak another day."

8:10 For if someone should see you with your knowledge, reclining in an idol-temple, won't their conscience, being weak, be built up to eat idol-meat? 11 So the weak one is destroyed by your knowledge – this brother or sister, for whom Christ died. 12 And thus, sinning against brothers and sisters and damaging their weak conscience, you sin against Christ. 13 Therefore, if food causes my brother or sister to stumble, I will not eat meat ever again, in order that my brother or sister might not stumble.

Reclining in an idol temple

Grave decorations from Ancient Corinth, depicting a person (left) and gods (right) reclining at a feast:

An inscription from the first or second century CE, which is an updated translation of a previous inscription from the fourth century BCE, illustrates the perceived danger associated with becoming involved in other religious cults from the perspective of the Zeus cult:

163 The refusal to speak is presented as a comical excuse.

Inscription: Sardis (first or second century)
In the thirty ninth year of Artaxerxes'
reign, this statue
was dedicated by Droaphernes,
son of Barakis, governor of Lydia,
to the Legislator Zeus. He commands those
who come into the
inner sanctum as temple wardens, to
serve and crown the God,
that they should not partake in the mysteries of Sabazios
with those who bear the burnt offerings;
and the mysteries of Angdistis and of Ma.
And Dorates the temple warden is commanded
to stay away from these mysteries.

9:1 Am I not free? Am I not an apostle? Have I not seen Jesus our Lord? Are you not my work in the Lord? 2 If to others I am not an apostle, I surely am to you – for you are the seal of my apostleship in the Lord.

Am I not free?
This depiction of *Libertas* on the reverse of this coin of Emperor Claudius (41–54 CE) illustrates the Roman value of "freedom" at this time. Paul claims to possess the freedom that the Corinthians admire, but emphasises that he chooses to give it up for the sake of others.

Have I not seen Jesus our Lord?
Paul's encounter with Jesus on the Road to Damascus is described in Acts 9 and 22.

9:3 This is my defence [ἀπολογία] to those who are judging me.

This is my defence
As in chapters 5–7, chapter 11, and chapters 12–14, Paul appears to move into an interlude here, before returning to a development of the theme of chapter 8 in chapter 10. This interlude on apostolic "rights" complements and illustrates that theme.

There is debate about whether Paul's use of the word "defence" here (cf. Acts 22:1) indicates that this chapter is essentially a rebuttal of the Corinthians' accusations, or whether the term is used less formally here.

Plato depicts Socrates giving a formal defence of charges that have been brought against him:

> *Plato: Apology of Socrates, 18e–19a*[164]
> Well then: It is necessary for me to make my defence [ἀπολογητόν], O people of Athens, and I must attempt to remove from you the deceit which you have held for quite some time – and I must do this in only a little time. I would like for it to turn out this way, if it is better both for you and for me: that I might succeed in making my defence. But this will be difficult, and this fact has not altogether escaped my notice. Nevertheless, let that which pleases God be done: the law must be adhered to. I will make my defence.

9:4 Do we not have the right to eat and drink? 5 Do we not have the right to bring along a believing wife, as do the rest of the apostles and the brothers of the Lord and Cephas? 6 Or is it only myself and Barnabas who do not have the right to refrain from work? 7 Who serves as a soldier at their own expense? Who plants a vineyard and does not eat of its fruit? Or who shepherds a flock and does not partake of the milk of the flock?

8 Am I saying these things on human authority, or does the law also say this? 9 For in the law of Moses it is written:

> **Do not muzzle a working ox.**

Is it oxen that are of concern to God, 10 or does he say this entirely on our account? For it is on our account that it is written:

> **The one who farms and the one who threshes ought to do so in the hope of sharing in the harvest.**

The right to refrain from work

Aristotle's comment below expresses the social distinction between benefactors and recipients, which still existed strongly in Paul's time. It may be that Paul has intentionally denied the Corinthians the opportunity to be his benefactors, because he doesn't want them to think that they can buy "superiority" or control over him. Whether or not this is the case, it seems that some in Corinth now want to discredit Paul's worthiness to receive payment at all. See also Cicero, *De Amicitia*, 14.51; *Ad Familiares*, 2.6.1.

[164] Socrates is presented as attempting to formally prove his innocence.

Aristotle: Nicomachean Ethics 4.3.24[165]
The great-souled person is pleased to be a benefactor, but ashamed to be on the receiving end: The former is superior, but the latter, inferior.

The honour associated with being a benefactor is illustrated in Josephus' praise of Agrippa:

Josephus: Jewish Antiquities, 19.330–331[166]
But Agrippa had a gentle manner, and acted as a benefactor to all equally. To those of other nations he was benevolent and showed his generosity to them, while showing proportionately more kindness and compassion to those of his own race.

The deference given by a recipient to a benefactor is illustrated in this letter from the first or second century:

Papyrus letter: Letter to Sarapion (first or second century CE*)*
Herm... and... Greetings, and may you always remain healthy in your whole body, for many years. Because of your kind fortune, you have allowed us to honour [προσκυνήσωμεν] and greet you. For just as you also remember us in each letter, so at this end I conduct worship for you before the lords Dioskoroi and before the lord Sarapis; and I pray for your wellbeing in all of life, and the health of your children and of your whole household. In everything, farewell, my patron and provider. Greet all of your men and women. All of the gods and goddesses here greet you. Farewell, Thoth 16th.

Dio Chrysostom reacts against the practice of groups seeking "wise" orators who will tell them what they wish to hear:

Dio Chrysostom: Discourses: First Tarsic Discourse, 33.4–5[167]
You seem to me to have often listened to amazing men, who say that they know all things, and, concerning these things, to know what their purpose and nature is – concerning humans and spirits and gods; earth and sky and sea; sun and moon and the other stars; the whole universe and mortality

[165] From Aristotle's perspective in this context, it is only those whose benefactions arise from genuine virtue that genuinely deserve honour.

[166] Josephus is describing the actions of Agrippa in the time of Claudius. Agrippa is described in very positive terms, in contrast to the previous king, Herod.

[167] This comes toward the beginning of a speech that resists the audience's preference for pleasing rhetoric.

> and generation; and innumerable other things. And it seems that they come to you and enquire about what you would like them to say, and in what way, in accordance with Pindar: "Ismenus, or Melia of the golden distaff, or Cadmus"! Whatever seems fitting to you, the speaker takes up, and pours out a full speech, like the release of a stream that had been dammed up within him! Then, when you hear him, it seems distasteful and untimely to closely examine each matter, or to disbelieve such a wise man. But rather, at the force and speed of his words, you are stirred up and you greatly rejoice, as he breathlessly combines a throng of words. And you are moved, like those who view the galloping horses. Although you benefit nothing, you are amazed and say what a blessing it is to have such a possession!

Paul is depicted as working in Corinth in Acts 18:1–3 (cf. 1 Thessalonians 2:9; 2 Thessalonians 3:7–9).

Who plants a vineyard and does not eat of its fruit?
It is possible that Paul is alluding to Deuteronomy 20:6 here, which concerns the right of Israelites to enjoy their inheritance rather than die in battle.

Do not muzzle a working ox
This is a quotation from Deuteronomy 25:4. The verb "muzzle" (κημώσεις) does not match the Septuagint. It is possible Paul and Sosthenes were working from memory here.

> *Deuteronomy 25:4, Septuagint*
> Do not muzzle (φιμώσεις) a working ox.

Is it oxen that are of concern to God?
Philo similarly argues that it is not for the benefit of animals that the law includes commands about animals, but rather for the benefit of humans:

> *Philo: The Special Laws, 1.260*[168]
> For the law is not concerned with irrational animals, but with those who have understanding and reason.

The one who farms and the one who threshes
This appears to be a proverbial expression (cf. 2 Timothy 2:6).

[168] In context, Philo is arguing that the law's demand for sacrificial animals to be faultless should be understood as symbolic of the necessary purity of the human who offers the sacrifice.

9:11 If we have sown spiritual seed among you, is it too much if should we expect a fleshly harvest from you? 12 If others have the right to share with you, don't we have more? But we have not used this right; rather we endure everything, in order that we might not provide any hindrance to the gospel of Christ.

13 Do you not know that those who work with the things of the temple eat their food from the temple; that those who serve at the altar share in the sacrificial meat? 14 So also the Lord has directed that those who proclaim the gospel should make their living from the gospel.

Those who work with the things of the temple
Deuteronomy 18 directs that the Levitical priests should eat the sacrifices offered to God rather than receive a regular inheritance.

9:15 But I have never used these rights. And I have not written these things in order that they might be given to me. For it would be better for me to die than to have my boast made empty by anyone. 16 For if I proclaim the gospel, this is nothing for me to boast about. For I am compelled to do it. Woe to me if I do not proclaim the gospel! 17 For if I do this voluntarily, I have a reward; but if not, I am simply discharging my responsibility. 18 What then is my reward? That, proclaiming the gospel without charge, I might not abuse my right in the gospel.

I have never used these rights
It seems that the Corinthians made much of their "rights" (6:12; 10:23), exemplifying a long standing Greco-Roman emphasis on the dignity of exercising one's liberties. Aeschines, for example, indicates that in Greek law (of an earlier period) a father who had denied the rights of his son would be punished by undergoing the dishonour of having his own rights removed:

> *Aeschines: Against Timarchus, 1.14*[169]
> See, O men of Athens, how well this fits: while the man is alive, he is denied the benefits of fatherhood, just as the son had been denied the right to speak publicly. But when he has died, being unable to perceive the good that is done for him, and when it is evidently the law and the divine that receive the honour, the son is urged to bury him and to do all the other appropriate customs.

169 In context, the situation in view is one in which a son who had been forcibly hired out as a child prostitute by his father was not obligated to look after the rights of the father, except for burial rights.

Such an emphasis on the honourable exercise of freedoms and rights – particularly for the elite – persisted in the Roman era. Paul's discussion here may be read as a subversion of such expectations.

Epictetus commends a Stoic resolve to defend God's providence, by cheerfully accepting the bad with the good:

> *Epictetus: Discourses, 2.16.41–2*[170]
> Lift up your neck, as one who has been released from slavery. Dare to look up to God to say, "Use the rest of my life for whatever you wish! I share your purposes. I am yours. I refuse nothing that seems good to you. Lead me where you will. Clothe me with the clothing that you choose. Do you want me to rule? To be private? To remain? To flee? To labour? To be wealthy? In regard to all these things I will defend you before the people: I will show the nature of each."

However, in distinction from this Stoic perspective, Paul expects to receive an eschatological "wreath" of victory at the end of his labour.

9:19 For, although I am free of all, I have enslaved myself to all, in order that I might win many. 20 And I have become like a Jew for those who are Jews, in order that I might win Jews: to those under the law I have become like one under the law – not being under the law myself – in order that I might win those under the law. 21 To those without the law I have become like one without the law – not being without the law of God myself, but subject to the law of Christ – in order that I might win those without the law. 22 To the weak I have become weak, in order that I might win the weak. I have become all things to all people, in order that by all means I might save some.

All things to all people
A variety of Jewish and Greco-Roman backgrounds has been suggested for this section.[171]

---

170 This is presented as a challenge to a lazy and unwilling interlocutor.

171 For a discussion of various possible backgrounds to this section, see Margaret M. Mitchell, "Pauline Accommodation and 'Condescension' (συγκατάβασις): 1 Cor 9:19–23 and the History of Influence" in Engberg-Pedersen, Troels (ed), *Paul Beyond the Judaism/Hellenism Divide* (Louisville, Westminster John Knox Press, 2001), 197–214; and chapter four of David J. Rudolph, *A Jew to the Jews: Jewish Contours of Pauline Flexibility in 1 Corinthians 9:19–23* (Tübingen, Mohr-Siebeck, 2011).

One suggestion is that Paul's "enslavement to all" may be read against the background of philosophical discussion of the "*polytropic man*" (especially associated with Odysseus).[172]

> *Theognis: Elegi, 213–15*[173]
> O Soul! Adopt different kinds of character according to all kinds of friends, mixing your mood with that of each. Have the mood of a complex polyp, which adjusts to the rock it is on.

Related to this is the *rhetorical topos of the enslaved leader*.[174] According to this reading, Paul presents himself as a (modified) recognisable model of the leader who willingly pursues enslavement to those he leads. Pseudo-Phocylides adopts the common rejection of (a caricature of) this model:

> *Pseudo-Phocylides: Sentences, 48–50*[175]
> Do not conceal a different thought in your heart while publicly speaking; do not be like the polyp on the rock that changes according to its environment. Be sincere to all, publicly speaking those things that are in your heart.

Another proposal is that Paul's adaptability develops *Jewish patterns of flexibility*.[176] Exodus 30:17–21 calls upon *priests* (not the laity) to conduct ritual handwashing; yet Mark 7:1–5 presents the (non-priestly) Pharisees as upholding handwashing as an essential tradition. That is, *though not priests, they become like priests at the table, in order to honour the law* (in accordance with the Traditions of the Elders). In other instances, it may be that the Pharisees' willingness to be lenient with regard to ritual purity (relative to the Sadducees and Essenes) aided their popularity with the people.[177] Perhaps Paul's accommodation arises from the development of such an orientation, and relates to his varying adoption of these very traditions in the company of ordinary Jews ("to the Jew"), Pharisees ("to those under the law"), and Gentiles ("to those without the

---

172 See Abraham J. Malherbe, *Paul and the Popular Philosophers* (Minneapolis, Fortress Press, 1989, 2006), 100, 119.

173 Here, Odysseus' character is presented in a positive light.

174 See Dale B. Martin, *Slavery as Salvation: The Metaphor of Slavery in Pauline Christianity* (New Haven and London, Yale University Press, 1990), chapters 3 and 4.

175 The wider section is about honesty, modesty, and self-control.

176 See David J. Rudolph's dissertation, mentioned above.

177 See Rudolph, 114–15. On the popularity of the Pharisees, see Josephus, *Antiquities*, 13.288–299.

law"). Thus according to this proposal, Paul's adaptability consists in a varying adoption of Pharisaic *halakha,* rather than a varying adoption of the *Torah* itself.

Philo indicates that *God* accommodates himself to the varying capacities of different souls, without changing his essential nature. It may be that Paul has a similar concept in mind:

> *Philo: On Dreams I 232*[178]
> To those souls that are incorporeal and in his service, he reveals his likeness to them as he really is – communicating as a friend to friends. But to those that are still in a body, he takes on the likeness of angels, not changing his own nature – for he is unchangeable – but taking on the form of a different manifestation for those who perceive him. And they receive that likeness not as a copy, but as the original form itself.

9:23 And I do all this because of the gospel, in order that I might become one who shares in it. 24 Do you not know that those who race in a stadium all run, but only one receives the prize? Run in the same way – in order to receive the prize. 25 Everyone who takes part in the games goes into controlled training, and they do so in order to receive a perishable wreath; but we aim to receive one that is imperishable. 26 This is how I run: not aimlessly; and this is how I fight: not beating the air. 27 But I beat my body and enslave it, in order that I might not proclaim to others, and yet become disqualified myself.

Those who race
Corinth was situated near two important centres of Greek games: Isthmia and Nemea. Indeed, Corinth itself hosted the Isthmian games for many years. Below are the locker room and stadium at Nemea (where Nero himself performed):

[178] Philo's point is about divine accommodation rather than human accommodation. It is possible, though, that this theme (which extended beyond Philo) was influential for Paul (cf. 11:1). See also Philo's discussion of divine and angelic accommodation in relation to table-fellowship with Abraham: *On Abraham,* 113.

Left are the remains of the temple of Poseidon at Isthmia:

Strabo: Geography, 8.6.4
Near Schoenus is the diolkos, at the narrowest part of the Isthmus, where the Isthmian temple of Poseidon can be found.

8.6.19
Here also is Nemea, in the middle of Cleonae and Phlius, and the grove in which also the Nemean Games are customarily pursued by the Argives . . . And we, from Acrocorinth, have spied the colony [of Cleonae].

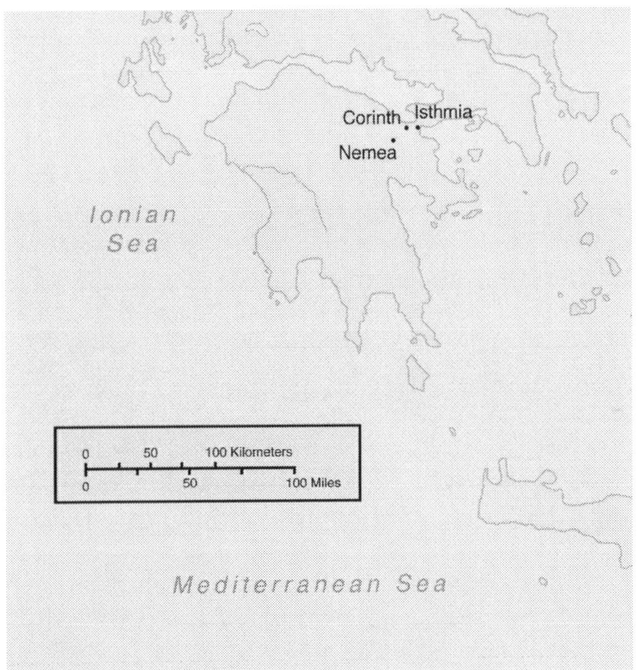

Below is the base for a prize that was won in Greek games of the first century, situated in the *agora* at Athens:

Controlled Training
Plato uses the imagery of the Olympics to make a similar point, indicating that even at this prior time, the arduousness of athletic training was known as a literary device (cf. Epictetus, *Discourses*, 3.22.52; 4.4.11–13; Seneca, *Epistles*, 78.16):

Plato: Laws, 840b–c[179]
Athenian: What then? If for the sake of victory in wrestling and racing and other such things, these people were able to endure abstinence from acts of so-called enjoyment, are our children unable to be patient for the sake of a greater victory – which is the most admirable, as we shall tell them from childhood, enthralling them with tales and words and songs?

A Perishable Wreath
Question 3 of book 5 of Plutarch's *Table Talk* gives some insight into Paul's imagery here. It begins:

Plutarch: Table Talk, 5.3[180]
Why is pine supposed to be sacred to Poseidon and Dionysus; and why was the victor at the Isthmian Games formerly crowned with a pine wreath, and later with wild celery, but now once again with pine?

10:1 I do not want you to be ignorant, brothers and sisters, that our ancestors were all under the cloud and all passed through the sea, 2 and all were baptised into Moses through the cloud and the sea; 3 and all ate the same spiritual food,
4 and all drank the same spiritual drink. For they drank from the spiritual rock that accompanied them – and the rock was Christ. 5 But God was not pleased with most of them, and they were overthrown in the wilderness.

Our ancestors were all under the cloud and all passed through the sea
In drawing a parallel between the experience of the ancestors and the "spiritual" practices of the Corinthian communities, Paul calls upon the well-known stories of exodus (Exodus 12), wilderness (Exodus 13), provision of manna (Exodus 16) and water from the rock (Exodus 17).

In the rehearsal of these foundational narratives in Psalm 105:39–41, the cloud is similarly pictured as a covering for the people of Israel. This is taken up in the *Wisdom of Solomon*:

Wisdom of Solomon 10:17[181]
[Wisdom] gave to these people a reward for their labours, and guided them in the path of wonders, and became for them a covering by day and a starry flame by night.

179 The Athenian is arguing that citizens ought to attain victory over the base desire for sexual pleasure.

180 This is the question that he then goes on to discuss. The relevance here is simply that the wreaths for the games are made of perishable material.

181 "Wisdom" is being depicted as actively involved throughout the history of Israel.

Wisdom of Solomon 19:7[182]
The cloud overshadowed the camp.

They drank from the spiritual rock
Both the *Wisdom of Solomon* and Philo mention the rock from which the Israelites drank in the wilderness as a sign of God looking after Israel by means of Wisdom:

Wisdom of Solomon 11:4[183]
They thirsted and called upon you, and you gave them water from the jutting rock, and satisfaction of thirst from the hard stone.

Philo, On Allegorical Interpretation, 2.86[184]
For the jutting rock is the wisdom of God, which is both transcendent and the first of the things he quarried by his own power. And he gives drink from it to the souls that love God; and when they have drunk, they are also filled with the most universal manna; for manna is that which is called the primary class of everything. But the most universal of all things is God; and in the second place the word of God.

The mention of Christ as the "rock" perhaps recalls Deuteronomy 32, where God is identified with the same image.

10:6 Now these things happened as examples for us, in order that we might not be associated with wicked desires, as they were. 7 Neither should we become idolators, as some of them did – as it is written:
The people sat down to eat and drink and rose up to play.

The people sat down to eat and drink and rose up to play
This is a quotation of Exodus 32:6, which describes Israelite idolatry. Paul's wording follows the Septuagint.

10:8 Nor should we practise sexual immorality, as some of them did – and twenty-three thousand fell in one day. 9 Nor should we put Christ to the test, as some of them did – and were destroyed by snakes. 10 Nor should we grumble, as some of them did – and were destroyed by the Destroyer.

---

182 The events of the Exodus are recalled in vivid imagery at this point.

183 This is part of a long section, showing how God consistently looked after Israel by means of wisdom.

184 Philo is giving a symbolic interpretation of the wilderness experience, whereby the bites of scorpions and snakes represent pleasure, and the refreshment of water represents God's wisdom.

Nor should we practise sexual immorality . . . put Christ to the test . . . grumble
Many of these themes appear in the book of Numbers. Numbers 16 describes grumbling; Numbers 21 describes death by snakes; Numbers 25 describes sexual immorality and the death of 24,000 (not 23,000).

Were destroyed by the Destroyer
The Destroying Angel is found in Exodus 12:23; 2 Samuel 24:16; 1 Chronicles 21:12 and 2 Chronicles 32:21. Wisdom 18:25 similarly mentions the "Destroyer" (ὁ ὀλεθρεύων) as the one who bears wrath and death.

10:11 But these things happened to them as an example, and were written down to be a warning for us, on whom the end of the ages has come. 12 So let the one who thinks they stand watch that they don't fall. 13 No temptation has overcome you except that which is human. God is faithful, and will not allow you to be tempted beyond that which you are able to stand – but will provide, alongside the test, a way out, so that you are able to endure.

These things happened to them as an example
Other Jewish writers use the example of Israel's past in order to exhort the present generation. Josephus is illustrative:

> *Josephus: Jewish War, 5. 390*[185]
> All in all, it may be said that there is no case in which our ancestors triumphed by use of weapons, or were defeated without weapons, when they turned to God.

For the same technique in Roman rhetoric, see Quintilian, *Institutes of Oratory*, 5.11.6.

No temptation has overcome you except that which is human
It may be that this refers to temptation that is "common to humanity". Alternatively, it may once again be expressing a distinction between that which is *human* (temptation), and that which is *divine* (faithful provision).

10:14 Therefore, my beloved, flee from idolatry. 15 I am speaking to you as to people who are sensible. Judge for yourselves what I am saying: 16 The cup of blessing that we bless: is it not a participation in the blood of Christ? The

185 Josephus is encouraging his fellow Jews to learn from Israel's history that they must not take it upon themselves to wage war against their occupiers.

bread that we break: is it not a participation in the body of Christ? [17] Because
there is one loaf, we who are many are one body – for we all share from the
one loaf. [18] Consider fleshly Israel: Are those who eat the sacrificial meat not
partners in the altar? [19] What then am I saying? That idol meat is anything, or
that an idol is anything? [20] Rather that the meat that is sacrificed is sacrificed
to demons, and not to God. I do not want you to become partners with demons.
[21] You are not able to drink from the cup of the Lord and the cup of demons;
you are not able to share in the table of the Lord and the table of demons. [22] Or
shall we provoke the Lord to jealousy? We are not stronger than he, are we?

Partners in the altar
In Greco-Roman religion, sacrificial meat could be cooked on an *eschara,* such as the one pictured left, situated at Eleusis:

Israelite priests had been commanded to eat the food sacrificed on the altar of the Lord (Leviticus 7:5–6).

That an idol is anything
It is insisted that idols are nothing in Isaiah 41–42, where they are ridiculed for being unable to act or foretell the future. The theme comes to the fore again in Isaiah 44.

Sacrificed to demons
This may allude to Deuteronomy 32:17, which pictures Israelite idolatry in similar terms.

The table of the Lord
In Malachi 1:7,12, the altar in the temple is referred to as the "table of the Lord".

Shall we provoke the Lord to jealousy?
God is presented as "jealous" with regard to foreign gods in Deuteronomy 32:16–21.

[10:23] "Everything is lawful" – but not everything benefits. "Everything is
lawful" – but not everything builds up. [24] No one should be self-seeking,
but rather all should be other-seeking. [25] Eat everything that is sold in the
marketplace, without making an investigation on the grounds of con-
science.

[26] For the earth and its fullness are the Lord's.

**27 If an unbeliever invites you to eat, and you want to go, eat everything placed
before you without making an investigation on the grounds of conscience. 28
But if someone says to you, "This is consecrated meat", do not eat it for the sake
of the one who told you, and for the sake of conscience. 29 But I am not speaking
about your own conscience, but that of the other person. For why should my
freedom be judged by another person's conscience? 30 If I partake with thanks,
why should I be maligned on account of that for which I give thanks?**

"Everything is lawful"
See the comments and parallels in relation to 6:12.

Sold in the marketplace
Pausanius describes some of the temples and idols found in the marketplace of Roman Corinth:[186]

> *Pausanius: Description of Greece, 2.2.6*
> The things worthy of speaking about in the city are still left from ancient times, many of which come from the latter [i.e. Roman] period of the city's prime. On the agora – where many of the temples are found – are Artemis, surnamed Ephesian, and a wooden Dionysus, covered in gold except for their faces.

Marble statue of Ephesian Artemis from the first century BCE (left); Roman statue of Dionysus/Bacchus (middle); Corinthian Mosaic of Dionysus from the second or third century CE (right):

The agora of Roman Corinth (with a reconstruction of the temple of Apollo on the right):

[186] See also John Fotopoulos, *Food Offered to Idols in Roman Corinth* (Tübingen, Mohr Siebeck, 2003).

Shops of Roman Corinth:

The Lechaion Road, leading to the agora (where the meat market was situated):

Hera, whose temple was adjacent to the temple of Octavia:

As can be seen by the scale of the map below, all of these elements were very close together in central Corinth:

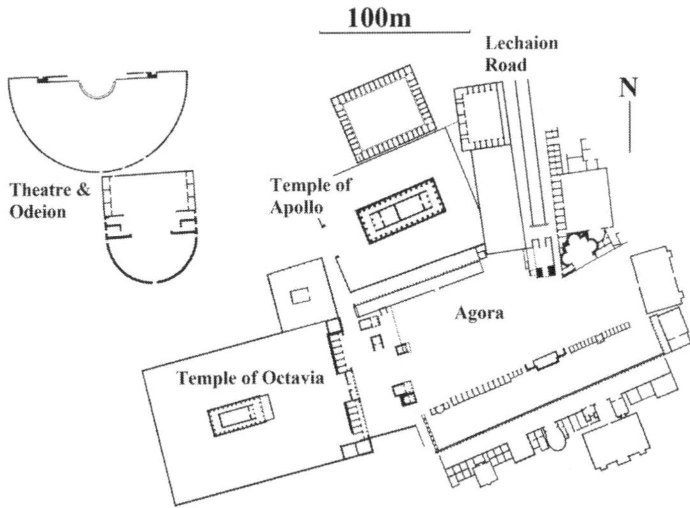

For the earth and its fullness are the Lord's
This is a quotation from Psalm 24:1. Paul follows the Septuagint.

10:31 Whether then you eat or drink, or whatever you do, do everything for the glory of God. 32 Do not become a reason for the stumbling of Jews or Gentiles or the church of God – 33 just as, in all things, I aim to please all people; not seeking to benefit myself, but to benefit many, in order that I might save them. 11:1 Become imitators of me, as I also am of Christ.

Become imitators of me
See comments in relation to 4:16.

11:2–11:34: Tradition and Division

2 I praise you that you remember all of my ways, and you hold the traditions, just as I passed them on to you. 3 But I want you to know that Christ is the head of every man, and man is the head of woman, and God is the head of Christ.

. . . and God is the head of Christ
This ordered list, in which the headship of *God* emphatically subverts human desire for esteem, carries a similar effect to 3:21–3 (cf. 11:12). It may be that the creation narratives in Genesis 1 and 2 are also significant.[187]

11:4 Every man who prays or prophesies with a covering coming down from his head shames his head. 5 And every wife [or woman] who prays or prophesies with her head uncovered shames her head – for it is just the same as being shaved bald. 6 For if a wife is not covered, let her also be shorn. But if it is shameful for a woman to be shaved or shorn, let her cover her head.

Every man who prays or prophesies

> *Plutarch: Roman Questions, 10*[188]
> Why, when they are praying to the gods, do they [i.e. Roman men] cover the head, and yet when they meet people worthy of honour while they have the *himation* on their head, they uncover it?

---

[187] The background of the word "head" here is fiercely debated. For a recent interaction with various perspectives, see Jerome Murphy-O'Connor, *Keys to First Corinthians* (Oxford, Oxford University Press, 2009), chapter 11.

[188] Plutarch deals with a variety of questions about why the Romans act in the way they do.

Roman men are often depicted as having their heads covered when engaging in religious worship. According to Plutarch, this headcovering (the *capite velato*) was expressive of humble devotion. It especially appears in depictions of those in respected positions of priestly leadership. It seems that Paul is hinting at this practice, although it cannot be established that Christians in Corinth were already acting in this way. The phrase κατὰ κεφαλῆς also appears in Esther 6:12 in the Septuagint, where headcovering is certainly intended (cf. Plutarch, *Moralia*, 200F).

Left are statues of the emperors Augustus (left) and Nero, from Rome, in priestly poses, with heads covered:

The two statues below are from Eleusis, and probably represent the emperors Nero (54–68 CE) and Tiberius (14–37 CE):

The bust right is of Nero, and is from Corinth, circa 60 CE:

Apuleius hints that it is possible but unusual for a man's head to be exposed when engaging in priestly rites:

> *Apuleius: Metamorphoses 11.30 (cf. 11.10)*[189]
>
> And so that I would not devote myself to his mysteries as one who was undistinguished, he made me one of the group of *pastophori*, and, indeed, he chose to bring me into the board of *quinquennales*. Finally, he again shaved my hair off completely and I joyfully carried out my duties in the priesthood established in the days of Sulla [i.e. the early first century BCE], not concealing or covering my baldness, but in every place having it exposed.

[189] This is the resolution of the work, providing a happy ending to the story of the man's adventures.

Every wife [or woman] who prays or prophesies
Philo reports that both men and women participated in the worship of the Therapeutae, an ascetic Alexandrian Jewish group, following the pattern of Moses the prophet and Miriam the prophetess (*The Contemplative Life*, 87–88).

Married women are generally depicted as wearing headcoverings in Greco-Roman artwork – especially in settings designed to highlight piety; but sometimes they are presented bare-headed, with their hair tied up:

In specifically Roman artwork, women are sometimes presented with bare heads; but headcoverings perhaps connote public married devotion.[190] Left are two busts of the Empress Livia (58 BCE – 29 CE), the wife of Augustus and mother of Tiberias.

Below on the left is one of the two *Kores* that once supported the telesterion in Eleusis, bearing the *kiste* of the Eleusinian mysteries on her uncovered head. Perhaps rumours of such mysteries (which were led by priestesses) fuelled confusion about the connotations of removing headcoverings for worship. On the right is a sleeping *maenad* from the time of Hadrian. These female followers of Bacchus/Dionysus were said to be driven by him into uncontrolled frenzy (cf. comments on "ecstatic" female religious practitioners in relation to 14:23). Perhaps Paul was concerned that suspicious visitors would interpret the worship of the Corinthian Christian women with such images in mind.

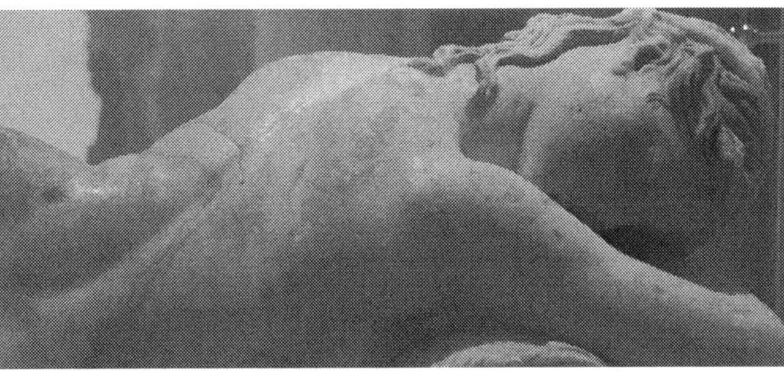

A number of ancient sources commend long hair for women and view it as shameful for a woman's hair to be loosed or removed. See Numbers 5:18; Philo, *Special Laws* 3.60; and the following:

> *Pseudo-Phocylides: Sentences, 210–212*[191]
> Do not allow locks [or braids] of hair to grow on the head of a male child.
> Do not braid his head or tie topknots on his head.
> For men, long hair is not fitting; but rather for ornate women.

[190] See David W.J. Gill, "The Importance of Roman Portraiture for Head-Coverings in 1 Corinthians", *Tyndale Bulletin* 41/2 (1990), 245–260.

[191] This occurs within a section about appropriate family relationships.

Sibylline Oracles: 3.359–361[192]
And many times your mistress will cut your beautiful hair, and as a punishment will throw you from above to the ground and get you back up again.

Aristophanes' play *Lysistrata* involves Greek wives giving advice to a magistrate, who can't bear the thought of taking advice from those who "wear veils". Clearly, for the magistrate, the veil represented a culturally recognisable role, which he believed the women were undermining:

Aristophanes: Lysistrata, Line 530[193]
Magistrate:
At your command, accursed one, I should be silent – you who have a veil covering the head? Not on my life!

In the play, it turns out that the women's contribution was essential to ending the war: the magistrate was a fool for doubting them.

11:7 For a man ought not to cover his head, as he bears the image and glory of
God. But woman is the glory of man. 8 For man is not from woman, but woman
from man. 9 For man was not created for woman, but woman for man. 10
Because of this the woman ought to have authority on her head – on account
of the angels [or "messengers": τοὺς ἀγγέλους] 11 Nevertheless neither woman
is apart from man nor man apart from woman in the Lord. 12 For just as woman
came from man, so also man comes through woman. But all come from God.

Man was not created for woman, but woman for man
This alludes to the account of the creation of humankind in Genesis 2.

On account of the angels/messengers
It may be that the tradition of the angelic "watchers" underlies the thought of this clause: According to this reading, Paul implies that angels watch or participate in Christian gatherings.

Book of the Watchers: 1 Enoch 6:1–2[194]
When the sons of men had multiplied in those days, lovely and beautiful daughters were born. And the angels, the sons of heaven, saw them and

---

192 This is an oracle of judgement on Rome.

193 At this point in the play, Lysistrata is urging the magistrate to take the wives' plan seriously. The magistrate is unconvinced. The wives go on to enact their plan, and finally peace is achieved.

194 This part of the *Book of the Watchers* elaborates on Genesis 6 (cf. 1QS 2:3–11).

said to one another, "Come, let us choose ourselves wives from the humans, and we will have children."

Alternatively, it may be that Paul means "messengers", in the sense of emissaries of the Roman empire[195] or from other churches.[196] Epictetus' reference to Cynics as messengers of the gods would be similar:

Epictetus: Discourses, 3.22.23[197]
It is necessary for the true Cynic to know that he is a messenger from God, sent to the people to show them about the things that are good and the things that are bad.

Discourses, 3.22.69
[The Cynic ought to be] the messenger and spy and herald of the gods.

11:13 Judge among yourselves: Is it proper for a woman to pray to God with her head uncovered? 14 Doesn't nature itself teach you that if a man has long hair it dishonours him, 15 but if a woman has long hair it is a glory for her? For long hair is given to her as a covering. 16 But if anyone seems to be contentious, we do not have any other custom – and neither do the churches of God.

Doesn't nature itself teach you
The argument from "nature" was often used to insist on a distinction between the sexes (and a corresponding rejection of homosexual practice):

Pseudo-Phocylides: Sentences, 190–194[198]
Do not transgress natural sex for irregular passion:
The beasts themselves are not pleased with homosexual intercourse.
Do not let women imitate the sexual role of men.
Do not let yourself become an uncontrollable torrent toward your wife.
For Eros is not a god, but a passion, destructive of all.

Josephus: Against Apion, II, 199[199]
And what of the laws concerning marriage? The law sees sex only as that according to nature with a woman; and this for the production of children.

195 See Winter, *After Paul Left Corinth*, chapter 6.
196 See Jerome Murphy-O'Connor, *Keys to First Corinthians*, 158.
197 The context concerns the need for the Cynic to be devoted to the service of God.
198 This occurs within a relatively lengthy section about sex and family relationships.
199 Josephus is commending Jewish laws relating to marriage.

But that of a man with a man it abhors, and punishes with death those who partake in it.

Josephus: Against Apion, II, 273[200]
The people of Elis and Thebes [were led to condemn] that which was against nature and unrestrained homosexual intercourse.

Josephus: Against Apion, II, 275
The Greeks attributed to the gods homosexual intercourse, and, for the same reason, marriage of brother and sister, that these might be a defence of their indulgence in unspeakable and unnatural pleasures.

Epictetus: Discourses, 1.16.12–14 Concerning Providence (cf. 3.1.25)[201]
Again, in relation to women, just as nature has produced something softer in the voice, so also she has taken away [facial] hair.... Because of this, we ought to preserve the symbols [of difference] given by God; we should not throw them away, or confuse, to the extent that we can, the distinctions between the sexes.

Musonius Rufus: Concerning Sexual Indulgence (Discourse 12)[202]
But of all sorts of intercourse it is the adulterous that are most unlawful, and of these, none is more immoderate than that of men with men, because such a reckless thing is against nature.

Musonius Rufus is especially interested in conforming to "nature" (as were Stoics more generally: cf. Epictetus 1.16.9–14), and so finds beards agreeable, as they are a "natural" covering for men. He advocates a distinction between the hairstyles of the sexes, and finds shaving contrary to nature:

Musonius Rufus: Concerning Cropping of the Hair (Discourse 21)[203]
Indeed, they carry themselves as androgynous, being seen as womanly, which ought to be fled from, by all means!

---

200 In this and the subsequent quotation, Josephus is demonstrating problems with the lax laws of the nations.

201 The point in context is to emphasise divine providence in nature, which should be respected.

202 This discourse explores sexuality from a Stoic perspective.

203 In this discourse, Musonius Rufus urges the retention of a natural distinction between the sexes when it comes to hair.

It is a glory for her
Achilles Tatius (*The Adventures of Leucippe and Clitophon*, 8.6) speaks of Leucippe's hair as her "crowning glory".

11:17 But in saying the following things I am not praising you, because you are not meeting together for better but for worse: 18 For firstly I hear that in your meetings together as a church, there are segmentations among you – and, in part, I believe it. 19 For it is necessary for there to be differences among you, in order that it might become clear who among you has been approved [δόκιμοι].

I am not praising you
The desire for praise and "approval", rather than shame, was very strong in Roman society. As the inscriptions from the Corinthian marketplace below illustrate, honour was given for accomplishment in civic, political, religious and competitive settings (which were not all clearly separated):

> *Inscription: White marble block found in the agora (39 CE)*
> To A. Arrius
> Aemilian Proclus,
> Augur, Chief Engineer,
> Aedile, Duovir, Imperial Priest
> Of Neptune;...
> Of the Tiberea Augustea
> Caesarea and Agonothete of the
> Isthmian and Caesarean
> Games.

> *Inscription: Marble statue base from the agora (Augustan)*
> To Sextus Olius Aemilian
> Secundus, Chief
> Engineer, Priest of Jupiter
> Capitolinus, Aedile and
> Duovir and Duovir Quinquennalis and
> President of the Games,
> By Decree of the Council.
> [Erected by] Sextus Olius Aemilian Proculus, son of Sextus
> And Cornelia
> After his death

Paul's insistence that he will not grant the Corinthians praise for their conduct when they "come together" may indicate that their segmentations at the common meal were an attempt to jostle for honour and praise.

Interestingly, this section on "not praising" (11:17–22) is set within a wider section of "praising" (11:2–34). As in the other subsections of this ethical portion of the letter (chapters 5–7; chapters 8–10; chapters 12–14), it appears that there is an ABA pattern here, in which the central section provides a complementary perspective.[204]

Aristotle had recommended that epideictic oratory (which may include praise and blame) ought to include digressions of praise:

> *Aristotle: On Rhetoric, 3.17.11*[205]
> And in epideictic, it is necessary for the speech to have episodes of praise, just as Isocrates does. For he always brings someone in. And this is what Gorgias used to say, that he was never left without something to say. For if he is speaking about Achillea, he also praises Pelea, then Aiakos, then God. Likewise also he praises courage, that it does this or that, or is like such-and-such.

Of course, oratory – and letter writing – had developed since Aristotle's time, but the practice of providing a complementary perspective as an interlude was not uncommon.

Who among you has been approved
See comments on "examination" and "approval" in relation to 11:28.

11:20 When you come together then, it is not the Lord's supper that you eat. 21 For each begins to eat their own supper – and one goes hungry while another gets drunk. 22 Do you not have homes at which to eat and drink? Or do you look down on the church of God, and shame those who have nothing? What shall I say to you? Shall I praise you? In this matter I have no praise for you!

---

[204] On the topic of oral communicative devices in Paul's letters, see John D. Harvey, *Listening to the Text: Oral Patterning in Paul's Letters* (Grand Rapids, Michigan, Baker, 1998). Note also Fee's reference to an ABA pattern (Fee, *First Corinthians*, 15–16) and Hurd's suggestion of a "sonata" form in Paul: "It seems to be characteristic of Paul that he will present an argument, then bring in a new theme, and finally re-argue the original topic in a new way. I call it Paul's 'sonata' form. When one begins to look for this pattern, numerous examples appear." Hurd, *Good News*, 61.

[205] In context, Aristotle is advising that speeches in praise of a certain person might do well to have digressions in praise of another.

One goes hungry while another gets drunk

The extent to which architecture played a role in the divisions at the Lord's Supper is debated. It is possible that houses that hosted church meetings only had room for the most elite members (or would-be elite members) to recline in the inner *triclinium* (which itself had conventional distinctions of status within its nine couch positions), while others would be located in the *atrium* or elsewhere. There is no clear evidence that the earliest Corinthian Christians maintained conventional usage of rooms for dining, but the possibility is worthy of consideration:[206]

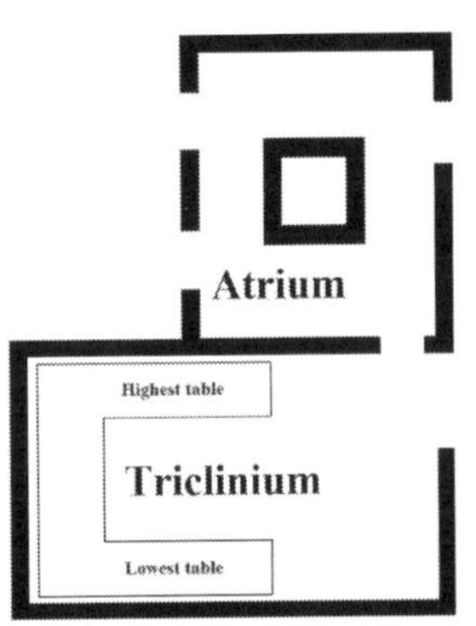

Internal decoration in a wealthy Roman house of the era:

Pliny the Younger illustrates the sort of culinary disparity that might accompany such a conscious division in status (cf. Martial, *Epigram* 3.60):

> *Pliny the Younger: Letter to Avitas (2.6)*[207]
>
> It would be a long story of incidental importance, to tell you in what way I came to dine with a certain man, with whom I am not very familiar. He thought himself to be at once lavish and economical, but he seemed to me to be both foul and gluttonous! For he set before himself and a select few the best dishes, while he set cheap morsels before the rest.

Philo hyperbolically depicts a contrast between Greco-Roman common meals and those of a contemplative Jewish group in Alexandria called the Therapeutae:

---

206 See the arguments in Jerome Murphy-O'Connor, *St Paul's Corinth: Texts and Archaeology* (Collegeville, Minnesota, *The Liturgical Press*, 1983 and 2002), as updated in *Keys to First Corinthians*, chapter 12.

207 In this letter, Pliny advises a young man against such a display of both extravagance and meanness.

Philo: The Contemplative Life, 40[208]
Now I would like also to mention their [that is, the Therapeutae's] common assemblies and the joyfulness of their symposia. For there are others who, when they have filled themselves with drink, behave as though it is not wine they have been drinking, but rather something herbal that causes frenzy and madness, and anything else that can be imagined that is more poisonous to reason. They cry out and rave in the manner of wild dogs, and they attack and devour one another.

44
And so those who, a little while ago, had come to the symposium as those who were sound and friendly, leave a little while later as enemies and with bodily injury.

48
And equally, some would approve the style of symposia now rife everywhere, through the pursuit of Italian expense and luxury, which is sought by both Greeks and Barbarians who desire show rather than celebration in making their preparations. Three-couch arrangements [*triclina*] or multi-couch arrangements, of tortoise shell or ivory…

11:23 For I received from the Lord that which I also passed on to you: That the Lord Jesus, on the night he was betrayed, took a loaf of bread, 24 and, having given thanks, broke it and said: "This is my body, which is for you. Do this in remembrance of me." 25 Similarly, he also took the cup after supper, saying, "This is the cup of the new covenant in my blood. Do this as often as you drink it, in remembrance of me." 26 For as often as you eat this bread and drink from this cup, you proclaim the Lord's death until he comes.

I received from the Lord that which I also passed on to you
Paul explicitly links the Corinthians' common meal with a tradition relating to Jesus' supper on the night of his betrayal. The history and shape of this common meal are debated. However, it would not have been at all unusual to share a common meal in the name of a god in Corinthian society. Perhaps Paul is displeased with certain ways in which the Corinthians are practising the "Lord's Supper" in the likeness of other common meals in Corinth.[209]

---

[208] Sections 40–47 of this work depict dissolute symposia, as a foil for his description of the common meals of the Therapeutae. The following sections, 48–52, emphasise the expensive luxury of Greco-Roman meals.

[209] See Hal Taussig, *In the Beginning Was the Meal: Social Experimentation & Early Christian Identity* (Minneapolis, Fortress Press, 2009).

The rules for the gatherings and cult meals of the Iobacchi are illustrative. Members gather together, according to agreed-upon guidelines, for eating, drinking, and performance of ritual:

> *Inscription: Athens (178 CE): Lines 42–47*[210]
> And the Iobacchi will gather together on the ninth of each month and on each anniversary and on each Bacchus-feast, and on any special feast of the god. And each member, whether speaking or acting or doing a good deed, will pay the decided monthly contribution for the wine.

The following stanza from a drinking song (*scolion*) was written on Egyptian papyrus in the first century CE, and would have been sung at communal meals as part of the *symposium*. The theme of the song appears to be the need to enjoy life while one has it:

> *Oxyrhynchus papyrus 1795.23*
> If ever you should see the dead, or pass by silent tombs,
> You are looking at the common fate of humankind; the one who is dead saw the same thing.
> Time is a loan, and the one who loaned you life is harsh.
> If ever he wants you to repay, you will do so lamenting.
> Play me a song!

This is my body

Paul has depicted Christ as "our Passover lamb" in connection with the discussion of unleavened bread in 5:7. He may expect that the Corinthians will be reminded of the role of "remembrance" of the Passover bread here (cf. Exodus 12:14; Deuteronomy 26:1–11; Jubilees 49:1–23; Josephus, *Antiquities* 2.317).

The cup of the new covenant in my blood

The theme of the "blood of the covenant" appears in Exodus 24:8. Jeremiah 31:31 promises a "new covenant".

You proclaim the Lord's death

Associations were expected to make a libation for the emperor in the context of their common meal. The fact that the Corinthians were rather called to make a libation ("drink from this cup") for one who had been *crucified* by the emperor was presumably supposed to be an act that was

---

[210] This inscription outlines the expectations for members of this association, including requirements for membership, payment, conduct, and worship.

starkly subversive of Rome's values.[211] It seems that some in Corinth needed to be reminded of this fact.

[11:27] So whoever eats the bread or drinks from the cup of the Lord unfittingly will be guilty of the body and blood of the Lord. [28] But let everyone examine themselves, and so eat of the bread and drink from the cup. [29] For those who eat and drink without discerning the body eat and drink judgement on themselves. [30] Because of this, many among you are sick and unwell, and some have fallen asleep. [31] But if we examine ourselves, we will not be judged. [32] But, when we are judged by the Lord in this way, we are being disciplined, in order that we will not ultimately be destroyed along with the world.

Let everyone examine themselves
"Examination" and approval before entering a sacred meal or assembly was not uncommon in the Greco-Roman world; although here, it is self-examination, rather than appraisal by a leader:

> *Inscription: Athens (second century* CE*)*[212]
> It is not lawful for anyone to enter this holy assembly
> of banqueters before being examined
> to see whether they are holy and godly and
> good.

We are being disciplined
The idea of God disciplining (rather than destroying) his people occurs in Deuteronomy 4:36; 8:5; 11:2; Job 5:17; Psalm 6:1; 38:1; 94:12; *2 Maccabees* 6:12–17; and *Wisdom of Solomon* 11:9–10.

[11:33] So, my brothers and sisters, wait for one another when you come together to eat. [34] If anyone is hungry, let them eat at home, in order that when you come together there will not be judgement – and I will give other instructions when I come.

Wait for one another
The general idea of relating to other participants of religious rites is broadly attested:

---

[211] See Taussig, *In the Beginning*, 131.

[212] This inscription outlines the expectations for members of this association, including requirements for membership, payment, conduct, and worship.

Dio Chrysostom: Fortieth Discourse: Delivered in his Native City on Concord with the Apameians, 40.28[213]
And consider… in relation to the common gatherings and festivals of the gods and spectacles, how much better and more prudent it is to mingle with one another in praying and sacrificing, rather than the opposite, cursing and maligning.

However, Paul's argument that the believers should show concern for one another here is theological, and specifically, participatory: The believers share in the body of Christ, and so should show concern for other members of the body.

12:1–14:40: Gifts and Love

12:1 Now, brothers and sisters, I do not want you to be ignorant about the spiritual. 2 You know that when you were Gentiles, whenever you were being led up, you were being led to speechless idols. 3 Therefore I want you to know that no one who speaks by the Spirit of God says, "Jesus be cursed!" and no one is able to say, "Jesus is Lord," except by the Holy Spirit.

You were led to speechless idols
That idols are speechless is emphasised in Psalm 115:4–5; Isaiah 44:9; Jeremiah 10:5; Habakkuk 2:18; and *3 Maccabees* 4:16.

Jesus be cursed! [or "Jesus, curse"]
Numerous "curse tablets" have been found in the vicinity of the cult of Demeter and Persephone in Roman Corinth, dating to the first century. The tablets request that the gods bring curses upon specific people, perhaps in retaliation after suffering some sort of offence. There is no evidence that the Christians in Corinth joined with this practice of making and burying curse tablets, but the concept of cursing one another in the name of a god may underlie Paul's statement here.[214]

12:4 There is a diversity of gifts, but the same Spirit. 5 And there is a diversity of services, and the same Lord. 6 And there is a diversity of works, but the same God works all in all. 7 To each, the manifestation of the Spirit is given for mutual benefit. 8 For to one, through the Spirit, a message of wisdom is given; while

---

[213] This is part of a speech urging concord between the cities of Prusa and Apameia.

[214] See the discussion in Winter, *After Paul Left Corinth*, chapter 8.

to another, a message of knowledge is given according to the same Spirit; [9] to another, faith, by the same Spirit; and to another, gifts of healing by the one Spirit; [10] to yet another, works of power; to another, prophecy; to another, the discerning of spirits; to another, speaking in other kinds of tongues; to another, the interpretation of tongues. [11] And one and the same Spirit accomplishes all of these, distributing each just as he desires.

To another, prophecy
This "manifestation of the Spirit" will be significant throughout chapters 12–14. The link between the Spirit and prophecy is well made in the Old Testament, and Joel 2:28 envisages the time when "sons and daughters" will have the Spirit and prophesy.

[12:12] For just as the body is one, and it has many parts, but all the many parts are one body, so also it is with Christ. [13] For by one Spirit we were all baptised into one body, whether Jew or Greek, whether slave or free, and we were all given the one Spirit to drink.

The body is one
The metaphor of a united multi-membered body is common in exhortations to interdependent unity in Greco-Roman literature:

> *Aristotle: Politics 8.1*[215]
> But it is necessary for those things that are public also to have public administration. But it does not thereby follow that we should suppose that any of the citizens belong to themselves. Rather, all belong to the city. For each is a part of the city. And the supervision of each part is achieved with regard for the supervision of the whole.

> *Maximus of Tyre: Oration 15.4–5*[216]
> But a city is something brought together by the joint work of all. The use of the body is similar, which itself has many parts and many requirements, and is preserved by the joint aim of the parts toward the corporation of the whole: Feet carry, hands work, eyes see, ears hear, and so on, lest I speak pedantically. But if the Phrygian story-maker wanted to compose a myth in which the foot, being fed up with the rest of the body, gave up, due to weariness, carrying and lifting such a heavy load, and pursued leisure and

[215] Aristotle's point is that because the city shares a common goal, education should be exercised with a view to the unity of the city's citizens.

[216] This is in the context of an argument for the advantage of active, practical involvement in society, rather than philosophical seclusion.

rest; or if the molars, because of grinding and producing food for such a crowd, grew angry, and, being asked, refused to give attention to their proper work – if these things happened at once, what other than the destruction of the person would ensue in the myth? This sort of thing is indeed what happens with regard to the political fellowship!

Often, however, the metaphor is used in order to preserve the role of the "greater parts" of the political body (cf. Livy, *The History of Rome*, 2:32, 7–11). Paul rather goes on to use the image to insist on the honour of the "less noble" parts.

12:14 For the body is not one part but many. 15 If the foot should say, "Because I am not a hand, I do not belong to the body," it would not, because of this, cease to belong to the body, would it? 16 And if the ear should say, "Because I am not an eye, I do not belong to the body," it would not, because of this, cease to belong to the body, would it?" 17 If the whole body were an eye, where would hearing be? If the whole were hearing, where would the sense of smell be? 18 But as it is, God has placed each one of the parts in the body, just as he wished.

The body is not one part but many

The image of many separate body parts may have reminded hearers of the Corinthian Asklepion, where images of various body parts were offered in gratitude for receiving healing from Asklepios, the god of healing (left):

If the foot should say . . .

Epictetus uses a similar image to make a different point:

Epictetus: Discourses, 2.5.26[217]

Why then are you bothered? Do you not know that just as the foot that has been removed is no longer part of the body, so if you are removed from society you are no longer a human? For what is a human? A member of the city.

12:19 If they were all one part, where would the body be? 20 But in fact there are many body parts, but one body. 21 And the eye is not able to say to the hand, "I have no need of you," or the head to the feet, "I have no need of you." 22 But,

[217] The point in context is that people should not consider their own trials in isolation from the whole society of which they are part.

rather, the parts of the body that seem to be weaker are essential; [23] those parts of the body which seem to be without honour, we treat with greater honour; and our less presentable parts we make even more presentable, [24] while our presentable parts do not need this.

The eye is not able to say . . .

A number of writers use similar metaphors to Paul here, considering whether one part of the body is more or less important:

> *Philo: The Special Laws 1.340*[218]
>
> Thus while each of the other bodily parts is present for a suitable and absolutely necessary use – such as the feet for walking and running and the other activities for which feet are suited, and hands for doing things and giving and receiving – the eyes are, as it were, for the common good, enabling the successful operation of these parts and all the others.

> *Dio Chrysostom: The First Tarsic Discourse, 33.16*[219]
>
> But something must have happened to you like that which Aesop says was suffered by the eyes. For, although they supposed themselves to be the most worthy bodily parts, they observed that the mouth gained pleasure from most things, and especially, honey, which is the sweetest. So they became angry and blamed the human [of which they were part]. But when that human placed honey on them, they felt pain and cried, and found it to be stinging and unpleasant.

[12:24] But God put together the body, giving greater honour to that which seems to lack it, [25] in order that there might not be divisions in the body but that each part might care for the others. [26] And when one part suffers, all the parts suffer together; when one part is glorified, all the parts rejoice together.

When one part suffers

Plato pictures the ideal city as being like a person whose various parts share one another's suffering and pleasure:

---

[218] This is part of an argument in which Philo is demonstrating that the senses may lead the soul to idolatry when confronted with idols.

[219] This is part of a speech that laments the moral decadence of the audience. The audience is here rebuked for wanting to be addressed only on their own terms.

Plato: Republic 5.10[220]
It is like when one of our fingers is hurt: The whole fellowship of bodily parts, which reach out to the soul to be an ordered unity under one ruler, perceives it. And the whole shares the suffering of the part at once. And this is how we can say that "the person" hurt their finger.

12:27 Now you are the body of Christ, and each is a member of it. 28 And God has placed in the church, firstly, apostles, secondly, prophets, thirdly, teachers, then wonders, then healing gifts, helping gifts, directing gifts, types of tongues. 29 All are not apostles, are they? All are not prophets, are they? All are not teachers, are they? All are not workers of powers, are they? 30 Not all have gifts of healing, do they? Not all speak in tongues, do they? Not all interpret, do they? 31 But seek the greater gifts.

And I will show you an even greater way. 13:1 If I speak in the tongues of humans and of angels, but I do not have love, I have become a resounding gong or a crashing cymbal. 2 And if I have prophecy and I understand all mysteries and all knowledge; and if I have all faith so as to move a mountain, but I do not have love, I am nothing. 3 And if I should give all I possess to the poor, and if I hand over my body to be burnt [or that I may boast], but I do not have love, I gain nothing.

I will show you a greater way
As in the other "rhetorical interludes" in the ethical portion of the letter, Paul here brings into focus a different perspective/embodiment of the issue at hand:

6:1–11: Lawsuits: The issue at hand is the unwillingness of the Corinthians to "judge" sexual immorality
9:1–27: Rights: The issue at hand is the Corinthians' exploitation of others on the basis of perceived rights and knowledge
11:17–22: Divisions: The issue at hand is the Corinthians' self-seeking enactment of ecclesial traditions
12:31–13:13: Love: The issue at hand is the Corinthians' self-absorbed attempts to express spirituality

As mentioned in relation to 6:1–11, the use of "interlude" is attested in Greco-Roman discourse.

---

220 Plato's interest here is in what makes for a well-governed state. It should not be thought that Paul is dependent on Plato here; simply that the image was a known literary convention.

Love

Plato similarly uses verse in extolling love:

> *Plato: Symposium 197c*[221]
> So it seems to me, O Phaedrus, that Love [that is, the god Eros] was firstly of surpassing beauty and goodness himself, and then was the cause of similar attributes in others. And I am compelled to say something in verse about him, as the one who makes:
> "Peace among humans, and stillness at sea
> A bed for the winds, and sleep for misery"

Paul's emphasis on love and his use of the noun ἀγάπη are more prominent than in the ethical sections of a number of other Jewish writers. In all of Philo's works there is but one reference to ἀγάπη, although he does urge that relational vices be avoided and virtuous harmony be pursued. At one point, Philo defines what it means "to love" in contrast to what it means to superficially "kiss":

> *Philo: On the One Who is the Heir of Divine Things VIII 40*[222]
> Now a kiss differs from love. For the one signifies the union of souls brought together in goodwill, while the other simply the bare superficial greeting.

Faith so as to move a mountain

This phrase appears to have been proverbial (cf. Mark 11:23).

13:4 Love is patient, love is kind, it is not jealous, it does not boast, it is not puffed up, 5 it is not uncouth, it does not seek for itself, it is not easily provoked, does not count wrongs, 6 does not rejoice at injustice, but rejoices at the truth; 7 it always bears up, always believes, always hopes, always endures.

8 Love never falls away. But where there are prophecies, they will be done away with; where there are tongues, they will be made to cease; where there is knowledge, it will be done away with. 9 For we know in part, and we prophesy in part. 10 But when the "complete" comes, the "in part" will be done away with. 11 When I was a child, I spoke as a child; I thought as a child; I reasoned

---

221 In this work, a variety of personas offer their thoughts on the nature of love. The speaker at this point is Agathon, who chooses to praise the god of love, rather than humankind's enaction of love.

222 The words for "kiss" and "love" are related in Greek. Philo clearly views genuine love as far surpassing the superficial.

as a child. When I became a man, I did away with the ways of childhood. [12] For now we see through a mirror, obscurely; but then, face to face. Now we know in part; but then we will know just as we are also known.

[13] But now remain faith, hope, love – these three. But the greatest of these is love.

Where there is knowledge, it will be done away with
Jeremiah 31:33–4 looks ahead to the time when the sharing of knowledge about God will be made redundant, as everyone will enjoy personal familiarity with God.

When I was a child
The imagery of (im)maturity is important throughout 1 Corinthians. At a number of points, Paul challenges those in Corinth to consider whether they will act as infants or as those who are mature.

Philo similarly uses the image of childishness to picture someone as captivated by worldly possessions:

> *Philo: On the Cherubim, 63*[223]
> For the story of Alexander of Macedon is that, when he seemed to have control of Europe and Asia, he stood in a prime position and, looking at the view around him, said, "The things in this direction and that direction are mine!", revealing the lightness of a soul that was both infantile and untrained, rather than kingly.

Here in chapter 13 of 1 Corinthians, however, the image seems to positively illustrate the distinction between necessary incompleteness in the present and the deferral of fullness to the future.

It may be that Paul's imagery ("obscurely"; "face to face") alludes to God's relationship with Moses, as pictured in Numbers 12:7–8 and Deuteronomy 34:10.

Now we see through a mirror
The image of the mirror draws attention to the ***indirect*** knowledge of God that characterises the present age. Philo uses the image similarly: A mirror gives a genuine, but reflected, view:

---

[223] Philo is illustrating the fall of Eve, in which sensory stimulation resulted in boasting.

Philo: On the Decalogue, 105[224]

Because of these things, and many others, the number seven is honoured. But nothing secures its prominence as much as the fact that by it, the maker and Father of all is most clearly revealed. For as through a mirror, the mind has an image of God acting and making the world and maintaining all things.

Faith, hope, love – these three

The mother in *4 Maccabees* is presented as exhibiting faith, hope, and endurance:

4 Maccabees 17:2–4[225]

O Mother, with your seven children, you destroyed the violence of the tyrant and extinguished his evil intentions and showed your noble character by your *faith*. For in *endurance* you nobly took your seat on the pillars of your children, without wavering through the tempestuous tortures. Take courage then, O holy-souled Mother, keeping the *hope* of endurance firm in God.

In the context of 1 Corinthians 13, it may be that the triad of verse 13 (faith, hope, love) presents an alternative focus to the triad of verse 8 (prophecy, tongues, knowledge).

**14:1 Pursue love, and seek the spiritual things; but even more, that you
should prophesy. 2 For the one who speaks in a tongue does not speak to
humans but to God; for no one understands, but with their spirit such a
person speaks mysteries. 3 But the one who prophesies speaks to humans
for up-building and encouragement and comfort. 4 The one who speaks in
a tongue builds up themself; the one who prophesies builds up the church.
5 Now I want all of you to speak in tongues – but more, that you should
prophesy. And the one who prophesies is greater than the one who speaks
in tongues without an interpretation – so that the church might receive up-
building.**

The one who speaks in a tongue

Speaking in language granted by the gods was not an unknown phenomenon in the Greco-Roman world. Sophocles' play *Ajax* is illustrative:

---

224 In the context of talking about why God created in seven days, Philo discusses the precedence of the number seven.

225 This comes in the context of a description of the mother's noble martyrdom.

Sophocles: Ajax, Lines 231–244[226]
Tekmessa:
Ah! So from there, from there to us
He came, leading his captive flock,
Some of which he slaughtered inside on the floor,
Others he cut in two from side to side.
He caught two swift-footed rams.
Of one, the head and the end of the tongue
He cut off and threw away. The other,
He bound upright on a straight pillar.
And taking a large horse-harness strap,
He struck it with the double whistling whip,
Abusing it with evil words that the spirits,
And not men, had taught him.

In the second century Jewish work *The Testament of Job*, Job's daughters are granted the ability to praise God in the language of angels:

Testament of Job 48:3[227]
And she spoke ecstatically in an angelic dialect, sending up a hymn to God, according to the hymnody of the angels.

It is by no means clear, however, that the believers in Corinth understood themselves to be speaking angelic languages.[228]

The one who prophesies builds up the church
The word "prophet" in the Hellenistic world appears to have especially designated officials at oracular sanctuaries, as illustrated in Plutarch's comments about the Delphic Oracles:

Plutarch: The Oracles at Delphi, 407d[229]
But he [the god] makes use of mortals as assistants and prophets [ὑπερέταις καὶ προφήταις], whom it is his duty to care for and guard, so that they are not killed by evil people while ministering to the god.

226 This is a report of the crazed spiritual influence with which Ajax was seized.

227 In context this speech is genuinely communicative, bringing glory to God.

228 See Christopher Forbes, *Prophecy and Inspired Speech in Early Christianity and its Hellenistic Environment* (Tübingen, Mohr-Siebeck, 1995), esp 187.

229 Plutarch is describing what used to happen for the people of "ancient days", when oracles were dispensed in an ambiguous way through the attendants.

Gillespie and Thiselton argue that regardless of Hellenistic practices, Christian "prophecy" should be thought of as applied exposition of the Christian *kerygma*. Forbes concurs that alleged parallels between Corinthian Christian prophets and so-called Hellenistic "ecstatic prophets" are not particularly enlightening here.[230]

The theme of "building up" has some background in the Old Testament, in which prophetic literature envisages the activity of "prophets" as God's means of "building up" God's people (e.g. Jeremiah 1:10).

But more, that you should prophesy
Moses is similarly depicted as wishing others to prophesy in Numbers 11:29.

The one who speaks in tongues without an interpretation
It may be that "interpretation" refers to the *articulation* of speech that is otherwise unintelligible to hearers.[231]

14:6 Now, brothers and sisters, if I should come to you speaking in tongues, how will I benefit you if I do not speak to you with a revelation or knowledge or prophecy or teaching? 7 It is similar with lifeless things that give sound – whether a pipe or a lyre: if no distinction between sounds is given, how will anyone know what is being played by the piper or the lyre-player? 8 And if the trumpet gives an unclear sound, who will prepare for war? 9 So it is with you when it comes to speaking in a tongue: if you do not give a clear message, how will anyone know what you are saying? For you are speaking into the air!

If you do not give a clear message
The necessity of clear and harmonious communication is at times a motif of Greco-Roman drama and political exhortation:

---

[230] Thomas W. Gillespie, *The First Theologians: A Study in Early Christian Prophecy* (Grand Rapids, Michigan, Eerdmans, 1994); Thiselton, "Meanings and Greek Translation Relating to 'Spiritual Gifts' in 1 Corinthians 12–14: Some Proposals in the Light of Philosophy of Language, Speech-Act Theory and Exegesis", in *Thiselton on Hermeneutics: Collected Works with New Essays* (Aldershot, Ashgate Publishing Limited; Grand Rapids, Michigan, Eerdmans; 2006), 335–347; Forbes, *Prophecy and Inspired Speech*, 208–217.

[231] Thiselton argues for evidence of this use of the word in Philo and Josephus: "The 'Interpretation' of Tongues: A New Suggestion in the Light of Greek Usage in Philo and Josephus", *Journal of Theological Studies* 30/1 (1979), 15–36; also, *First Corinthians*, 988.

Aeschylus: Prometheus Bound, 609–612[232]
Prometheus:
I will tell you plainly all that you need to learn,
Not twisting together obscurities, but in simple speech,
As it is right to speak openly to friends.
I am the one who gave fire to humankind – you are looking at Prometheus!

Dio Chrysostom: Discourses: On Concord in Nicea, 39.3[233]
As for me, I am pleased to see that you have unity of appearance, and speak with a common voice, desiring the same things.

The use of the trumpet in battle is illustrated in Numbers 10:9.

14:10 Even if there are many sorts of languages in the world, none of them is without sound. 11 If then, I should be unaware of the intent of the sound, I will be a foreigner to the one speaking, and the one speaking will be a foreigner to me. 12 So it is also with you: since you are zealous for things of the Spirit, seek to excel in those things that will result in the up-building of the church.

I will be a foreigner to the one speaking
Philo reflects on the confusion of tongues that occurred at Babel, and ponders the foreignness that comes from varied languages:

Philo: On the Confusion of Tongues, 13[234]
And if someone should acquire a number of languages, they will immediately be esteemed by those who speak them, as though such a person is already their friend.

14:13 Therefore the one who speaks in a tongue should pray that they might interpret. 14 For if I pray in a tongue, my spirit prays, but my mind is fruitless. 15 What then? I will pray with my spirit; but I will pray also with my mind. I will sing with my spirit; but I will sing also with my mind. 16 Otherwise if I should bless God in my spirit, how can others, who have the place of an outsider, say the amen to the thanksgiving – seeing as they do not know what you are saying? 17 It is good for you to give thanks, but the other is not built up. 18 I

---

232 Prometheus here explains the reality of his identity and suffering.

233 The context is a speech that urges concord.

234 Philo is demonstrating that uniformity of language is preferable to diversity of language. He goes on to ask why God wished to deprive humankind of a uniform language.

thank God that I speak in tongues more than all of you. [19] But in church I would rather speak five words with my mind in order that others might be helped, than ten thousand words in a tongue.

I will pray with my spirit; but I will pray also with my mind
Philo depicts ecstatic religious experience as involving the emptying of the human mind:

> *Philo: Who is the Heir of Divine Things 265*[235]
> And this is what occurs with the prophetic bands. For the mind, which is in us, is vacated at the appearance of the divine spirit. And it returns when the spirit departs. For it is a fundamental law that the mortal cannot dwell together with the immortal.

[14:20] Brothers and sisters, do not become children in your thinking, but become infants with regard to evil; in your minds become mature. [21] In the law it is written:

> **"In other tongues and with other lips I will speak to this people, and even then they will not listen to me, says the Lord."**

[22] So tongues are a sign not for those who believe, but for unbelievers – and prophecy is not for unbelievers but for believers. [23] If then the whole church were to come together, and all spoke in tongues, and an outsider or unbeliever came in, would they not say that you are out of control? [24] But if all were prophesying and an unbeliever or outsider were to come in, they would be convicted by all, brought under judgement by all, [25] having the secrets of their heart revealed. And thus, falling on their face, they will worship God, declaring "Truly, God is among you!"

In other tongues and with other lips
This is an adaptation of Isaiah 28:11–12. Paul's wording is dissimilar to both the Septuagint and the Hebrew. It would seem that, just as foreign languages were a sign of impending judgement in Isaiah, so Paul envisages that uninterpreted tongues in the Corinthian congregation will result in the ultimate "judgement" of unbelievers, who will have no opportunity to understand. Thus tongues are a "sign for [creating] unbelievers". Correspondingly, just as Isaiah's own prophecy brought the possibility of repentant belief, so the exercise of prophecy in Corinth will bring the possibility of repentant belief. Thus prophecy is a "sign for [creating] believers".

---

[235] Philo is defining prophecy as that which is utterly external to the prophets themselves.

Isaiah 28:10–12, Septuagint
You receive ordeal upon ordeal, hope upon hope – a little of this, a little of that – because of the contemptuous words that come through lips of other tongues. Because they will speak to this people, saying to them, "This is refreshment for the hungry and that is ruin" – but they do not want to hear.

Would they not say that you are out of control?
It may be that Paul's wording here alludes to the ecstatic behaviour involved in certain Greco-Roman cults:

Euripides: The Bacchae, 912–17[236]
Dionysus:
You, who are so eager for those things that you should not see,
And hasty for that which should not be pursued – I speak of Pentheus –
Come out in front of the house; show yourself to me!
You who have the outfit of a woman, of an ecstatic Bacchus attendant
[a *maenad*],
Spy of your mother and her group;
You come across in appearance like one of the daughters of Cadmus!

Wisdom of Solomon 14:27–8
For the worship of anonymous idols is the beginning and cause and conclusion of every kind of evil. For they rave in celebrations or prophesy lies or live unrighteously or swear hastily.

"God is among you!"
This echoes Isaiah 45:14, where the Gentiles are pictured as turning to God.

14:26 What then, brothers and sisters? Whenever you gather together, each has a psalm, or teaching, or a revelation, or a tongue, or an interpretation. Let everything happen for up-building. 27 If anyone speaks in a tongue, two or at the most three may speak one at a time, and one must interpret. 28 But if there is no interpreter, let them be silent in church, but let them speak by themselves to God.

Each has a psalm, or teaching, or a revelation, or a tongue
Synagogue meetings, Essene worship, and Greco-Roman association meetings were often more ordered than the rather free picture that this

236 Dionysus is referring to the groups of "ecstatic" female Bacchus attendants (*maenads*), which included women of all ages, engaging in apparently bizarre behaviour.

paints (see Josephus, *Jewish War* 2.8.6; 1QS 6:8–10; and Iobacchi inscription below). Paul does not offer an unqualified endorsement of this approach to congregational worship however; indeed, he immediately seeks to subject it to ordering for the sake of mutual edification.

14:29 Let two or three prophets speak, and the others should weigh it up. 30 And if a revelation comes to another, who is seated, the first should be silent. 31 For you are all able to prophesy one at a time, in order that all might learn and all might be encouraged. 32 And the spirits of prophets are subject to the prophets, for God is not a god of disorder but of peace.

As in all of the churches of the saints, 34 women (or wives) should remain silent in the churches. For it is not permitted for them to speak, but they should be submissive, just as the law says. 35 And if they want to learn, let them ask their own husbands at home. For it is shameful for a woman to speak in church. 36 Or did the word of God originate with you? Or has it reached you alone?

Let them be silent

Paul calls uninterpreted tongues-speakers, interrupted prophets, and interjecting women to silence.[237] The value of order and quietness was not unique to Christian religious gatherings. The rules for the gatherings of the Iobacchi state:

> *Inscription: Athens (178 CE) Lines 63–67*
>
> And nobody at the sacrificial ceremony is allowed to sing or cheer or clap; but, with all good order and quietness, should speak or act their part, under the direction of the priest or chief-Bacchus.

The spirits of prophets are subject to the prophets

This appears to be at variance with Philo's conception of (ecstatic) prophecy:

> *Philo: Who is the Heir of Divine Things, 266*[238]
>
> For indeed, the prophet, even when he seems to speak, in truth remains inactive, while another uses his speech organs, mouth, and tongue, to express whatever he chooses. With skill, invisibility, and musicality, this "other" plucks tunes and chords, and produces every harmony.

---

[237] The textual integrity of 14:33b–35 is questioned by Fee: *First Corinthians*, 699ff.

[238] Philo is insisting that the divine spirit displaces the human mind in the activity of ecstatic prophecy.

Let them ask their own husbands
Plutarch sees it as proper that women should speak to, or through, their husbands:

> *Plutarch: Advice to Bride and Groom, 142/32*[239]
> For a woman should speak to her husband or through her husband, and she should not be upset if she has a better voice through the tongue of another – as does the flute player.

14:37 If anyone thinks that they are a prophet or spiritual, let them acknowledge that the things I am writing to you are the Lord's command. 38 And if anyone ignores this, let them be ignored.

39 So, my brothers and sisters, seek prophecy and do not hinder the speaking of tongues. 40 But let everything be done in a fitting and orderly way.

---

[239] Plutarch is giving guidance about what will be considered virtuous for the newly married couple.

Present Death and Future Resurrection

Excursus: Chapter 15 and Reversal

The idea of a final reversal, in which the righteous are vindicated, and the boastful rulers are punished, is a very important theme in early Jewish literature. The "rulers" who were introduced in the opening chapters of 1 Corinthians as those who "crucified the Lord of glory" are now shown to ironically receive condemnation by the one whom they rejected.

It may be that the whole of 1 Corinthians is intentionally structured by this common pattern of reversal, in order to summon the Corinthians to trustingly follow the path of the presently-scorned but ultimately-vindicated Messiah, rather than the values of the presently-powerful but ultimately-condemned Roman elite.

The biblical Psalms of Lament (e.g. Psalms 22 and 30) frequently envisage a reversal of fortunes for the boastful persecutors and the faithful oppressed. The Qumran community similarly utilise this sort of rhetoric in their own Psalms, thanking God for reversal that has already been achieved, and expecting God to act as the great Reverser:

> *Qumran Thanksgiving Psalm: 1QH, Column 2, Lines 20–30*[240]
> I thank you Lord, for you have placed my life among the living
> And you have protected me from all the traps of the pit.

[240] This Psalm exhibits the sectarian self-understanding of the Qumran community: they are the righteous few, opposed by evildoers in the last times. They look to God as the one who brings down the evildoers and vindicates the righteous. The text of the Psalm is in very reliable condition.

For the violent have sought my life,
While I have held onto your covenant.

But these people are a council of wickedness and an assembly of Belial.
They did not know that my standing comes from you,
And that, in your mercy, you saved my life –
For my steps come from you.

And these people have fought against my life because of you,
So that you might be glorified in the judgement of the ungodly,
And, in me, you might be shown to be mighty, before the children of men.
For my standing is in your mercy.

And as for me, I said: "Mighty men have encamped against me,
They have surrounded me with all their weapons of war.
And arrows have broken without healing,
And the flaming spear has consumed the trees.

And like the roar of many waters is the commotion of their voice;
A rainstorm that destroys many.
Crushing through the cosmos, they bring about great wickedness
With the dashing of the waves."

And as for me, when my heart had melted like water,
You strengthened my life in your covenant.
But as for these people, the net that they spread for me will capture their own feet,
And they have fallen into the traps that they set for me.
But my feet stand in uprightness. In the assemblies I will bless your name.

The *Wisdom of Solomon* utilises this sort of rhetoric, calling the wise to inhabit the position of the humble righteous, rather than the arrogant ruler. As in Isaiah 53, the former boasters express shocked repentance as they witness the vindication of the faithful sufferer:

Wisdom of Solomon 5:1–8[241]
Then the righteous one will stand with much boldness, in view of those who had oppressed him, and those who had disregarded his labours.

[241] At this point, *Wisdom* looks ahead to the post-mortal experience of both the righteous and their ungodly persecutors, indicating a final reversal of fortunes.

> Seeing him, they will be stirred up with severe fear. And they will be amazed by the unexpectedness of his salvation. They will speak to one another in repentance, and from a spirit of distress they will groan and say, "This is the one whom we once held to be a laughingstock and an insulting byword – we fools! We considered his life to be madness and his death to be dishonourable. How is it that such a person has been counted among the sons of God, with an inheritance among the saints? So we had strayed from the way of truth, and the light of righteousness did not shine on us, and the sun did not rise for us. We were filled with lawless and destructive ways and travelled through inaccessible deserts, but we did not know the way of the Lord. Of what benefit to us was arrogance? And of what help to us was wealth with false pride?"

Likewise, the *Epistle of Enoch* calls the dead to wait and trust in the God who will bring reversal:

> *1 Enoch 102:4–5*[242]
> Be courageous, souls of the righteous who have died – souls of the righteous and godly – and do not grieve that your souls have descended into Hades with grief and your body of flesh has not been treated in accordance with your holy ways in your life.

3 Maccabees pictures God as the one who accomplishes reversal on behalf of his long-suffering people:

> *3 Maccabees: 7:21–23*[243]
> And, before their enemies, they [the formerly-persecuted but now-vindicated Jews] were held in greater esteem, with honour and fear, not having their possessions wrested by anyone. And everyone recovered all of their possessions, in accordance with the registration, so that any who had them returned them with great fear. The Most High God perfectly accomplished great things to bring about their salvation. Blessed be the Rescuer of Israel, for all time. Amen.

Josephus seems to see himself as a modern-day Jeremiah in *Jewish War*, and calls his fellow Judeans, in the midst of rebellion against the Romans, to recall that God sometimes gives power to other nations for his own

[242] This comes toward the end of the *Epistle*, in a section that looks ahead to the judgement of the sinners and the vindication of the righteous.

[243] This is the conclusion of the story, showing the final outcome as one of vindication.

wise purposes. He rehearses a number of moments in Israel's corporate memory, indicating that in each instance, God redeemed his people when they waited for his reversal:

> *Josephus: Jewish War, 5.382–383*[244]
> Should I mention the migration of our ancestors to Egypt? Though they were oppressed and made subject to foreign rulers for four hundred years, and could have defended themselves with weapons and violence, didn't they turn to God? Who does not know about Egypt being filled with all manner of beasts, and perishing with all manner of disease, the fruitless land, the failing Nile, the ten successive plagues, and how because of these things our ancestors were sent out with a guard, without bloodshed, without risk, as God led his holy people?

This hope for reversal can be seen in the *Testament of Judah*, employing imagery that resonates with 1 Corinthians:

> *Testament of Judah 25:4*[245]
> And those who have been killed by grief will be raised up in joy. And those who are in poverty on account of the Lord will be made rich. And those who are hungry will be satisfied. And those who are in a state of weakness will become strong. And those who have died because of the Lord will be awakened to life.

Indeed, the very identity of God and Israel are frequently related to the pattern of divinely granted reversal. Philo follows Deuteronomy 26 in indicating that worshipping Israelites were able to sum up the history of Israel as one of persecution followed by vindication:

> *Philo: Special Laws, 2.217–219*[246]
> This is the sense of the song: "The originators of our race left Syria and migrated to Egypt. Being few in number, they grew to become a nation of many people. Their descendants underwent numerous sufferings at the hands of the land's inhabitants; and when it was apparent that there could be no further aid from humans, they became pleaders before God, seeking refuge in his help. Their pleas were accepted by the one who is kind to all those who suffer injustice; and he entangled their oppressors with signs and wonders

---

[244] This is part of an extended argument from various moments in Israel's history.

[245] This is part of the conclusion of this *Testament*, looking ahead to final resurrected vindication.

[246] At this point, Philo explains a number of feasts and regular ceremonies.

> and strange phenomena and all the other spectacles that occurred at that time. And those who were being abused, and attacked by every evil desire, he rescued. And he not only brought them into freedom, but also gave them a fertile land. From the fruits of this land, O Benefactor, we bring you the firstfruits."

There are similar interpretations of Israel's history – with a movement from deathly persecution to divine vindication – by Achior in Judith 5, Eleazar in *3 Maccabees* 6, and Stephen in Acts 7.

Similarly, Paul now envisages the time when the "enemies" will be brought down and the "dead" will be raised. Notably, the "enemies" in 1 Corinthians 15 are not characterised as particular humans, but as "powers" and "Death" itself.

15:1 Now I want to remind you, brothers and sisters, of the gospel that I proclaimed to you, which you received, in which you have stood, 2 and through which you are being saved if you hold to the message I proclaimed to you – unless you have come to believe in vain! 3 For I handed on to you, as of foremost importance, that which I also received: That Christ died for our sins according to the scriptures, 4 and that he was buried, and that he was raised on the third day according to the scriptures, 5 and that he appeared to Cephas, then to the Twelve, 6 then he appeared to more than five hundred brothers and sisters at once, of whom most remain alive to this day, but some have fallen asleep. 7 Then he appeared to James, then to all of the apostles. 8 And last of all, as to one who had been miscarried, he appeared also to me.

Now I want to remind you
This phrase abruptly moves the letter into a very different section. The movement of this chapter may represent Paul's utilisation of micro-rhetoric. The examination of Paul's argumentation in this chapter usually recognises discrete sections as follows:[247]

1–11: The resurrection of Christ
12–19: The denial of the resurrection
20–28: The consequences of Christ's resurrection
29–34: Arguments from Christian experience
35–49: The resurrection body

247 This particular wording is an adaptation from Leon Morris, 1 Corinthians (Nottingham, IVP Academic, 2008).

50–57: Victory over death
58: Conclusion for the Corinthians

These divisions are largely agreed upon, although they may be said to express *topical* organisation (Holleman,[248] Garland,[249] Johnson[250]), *conventional rhetorical* organisation (Watson,[251] Witherington,[252] Thiselton,[253] Wegener),[254] or *chiastic* organisation (Welch,[255] Hull,[256] Bailey).[257]

If the movement of the chapter represents a form of conventional Greco-Roman micro-rhetoric, the sections above may be thought of as *Narratio* (1–11); *First Refutatio* (12–19); *First Confirmatio* (20–28; 29–34); *Second Refutatio* (35–49); *Second Confirmatio* (50–57); *Peroratio* (58).

He was raised on the third day according to the scriptures
Paul's Scriptures nowhere explicitly indicate that the Christ will die and be raised on the third day. However, as described above, there is certainly an established pattern whereby Israel, or its faithful representatives,

---

[248] Joost Holleman, *Resurrection & Parousia: A Traditio-Historical Study of Paul's Eschatology in 1 Corinthians 15* (Leiden, Brill, 1995).

[249] David E. Garland, *1 Corinthians* (Grand Rapids, Michigan, Baker Academic, 2003).

[250] Andrew Johnson, "Firstfruits and Death's Defeat: Metaphor in Paul's Rhetorical Strategy in 1 Cor 15:20–28", *Word & World* 16/4 (1996), 456–464; "Turning the World Upside Down in 1 Corinthians 15: Apocalyptic Epistemology, the Resurrected Body and the New Creation", *Evangelical Quarterly* 75/4 (2003), 291–309.

[251] Duane F. Watson, "Paul's Rhetorical Strategy in 1 Corinthians 15", in Porter, Stanley E; Olbricht, Thomas H. (eds), *Rhetoric and the New Testament: Essays from the 1992 Heidelberg Conference* (Sheffield, Sheffield Academic Press, 1993, 2001).

[252] Witherington III, *Conflict and Community*, 291–2.

[253] Thiselton, *First Corinthians*, 1177–8.

[254] Mark I. Wegener, "The Rhetorical Strategy of 1 Corinthians 15", *Currents in Theology and Mission* 31/6 (2004), 438–455.

[255] John W. Welch, "Corinthian Religion and Baptism for the Dead (1 Corinthians 15:29): Insights from Archaeology and Anthropology", *Journal of Biblical Literature* 114/4 (1995), 661–82.

[256] Michael F. Hull, *Baptism on Account of the Dead (1 Cor 15:29): An Act of Faith in the Resurrection* (Leiden, Brill, 2006).

[257] Kenneth E. Bailey, *Paul Through Mediterranean Eyes: Cultural Studies in 1 Corinthians* (Downers Grove, Ill.: IVP Academic, 2011), 421.

undergoes suffering, persecution and possible death before being vindicated by God. Many Psalms of lament follow this pattern (such as Psalm 22 and Psalm 30), as well as Isaiah 53, Ezekiel 37, narratives within Daniel, and the books of Job and Esther. Indeed, it is notable that here Paul uses the plural "according to the scriptures".

It may be that "the third day" was an idiom that indicated the expected end of a certain sequence. So Hosea 6:2 expresses that Israel will be "raised up" on the "third day", after suffering for a while. Luke has Jesus using the same idiom to speak about the necessity of reaching Jerusalem: "I am casting out demons and conducting healings today and tomorrow; and on the third day I will reach the goal" (Luke 13:32). The "Gabriel Revelation" also seems to utilise the number 3 in relation to (metaphorical) days, perhaps confirming its use as an idiom in first century Judaism:

> *Inscription: "The Gabriel Revelation"*[258]
> Line 19: Holiness for Israel! In three days you will know
> Line 54: …three days…
> Line 80: In three days… I, Gabriel

Perhaps, then, Paul believes that "the scriptures" were being fulfilled with the resurrection of Jesus on the third day in the sense that the scriptures envisaged the necessary vindication of the righteous representative of Israel.

Some have fallen asleep
The issue of "the dead" has been important throughout the letter: In the opening chapters, Paul emphasised that his gospel was about "Christ and him crucified", and he urged the Corinthians to imitate his own lifestyle as one "appointed to die". The references here to some who "have fallen asleep" and "one who had been miscarried" hint at the same theme, and are provocative in the context of a resistance to the revival of "the dead" in the Corinthian communities.

Depictions of death in Greek tombstones of the era are generally devoid of explicit hope, rather expressing the separation of the living and the dead. Note the downcast faces and the reaching of the living for the dead, or the dead for the living, in these examples from Athens:

---

[258] The context and meaning of these lines is hard to determine. It seems that the phrase "three days" is important in the 87 line Hebrew inscription; but beyond this, not much is certain.

Pausanius: Description of Greece, 2.2.4
And as one goes up to Corinth, there are tombs along the road.

However, in many Roman considerations of death in this period, there is a cautious, but vague, optimism:

Plutarch: Letter to Apollonius, 120/34[259]
And if the message of the ancient poets and philosophers is true, as it is likely to be, then also to the godly person who has departed, there is honour and priority, just as it is said, and a place separated off in which these souls can pass their time – and so you ought to hold good hope for your late son, that he will be numbered among them.

Inscription: Gravestone of Roman Corinth
Tomb, you cover Timarchos' beloved daughter Kalaino, and with her an abundance of divine goodness. But an evil disease covered up the life of a

[259] This is from a genuine letter of condolence.

> good woman, before she met loathsome old age. And if, for those who are good, there is any honour under the earth, she has now attained first place with fair-breasted Persephone.

As to one who had been miscarried

In Numbers 12:12, Miriam's leprous state is likened to the appearance of a miscarried foetus. Philo hears this as a terrible insult, and uses the image in *Allegorical Interpretation 1.76* to depict the malformed and deathly desires of the worthless soul. Paul's adoption of this image for himself would no doubt have come across as jarring, evoking the image of death as much as, if not more than, the *timing* of Jesus' appearance to him.

15:9 For I am the least of the apostles, unworthy to be called an apostle, because I persecuted the church of God. 10 But by the grace of God I am what I am, and his grace toward me has not been in vain, but I laboured more than all of them – not I, but the grace of God that was with me. 11 Whether then it was I or they, this is what we proclaimed and this is what you believed.

I laboured

Laborious toil would not have been esteemed as noble in Roman Corinth, as already noted in relation to 4:12. Further, *The Life of Adam and Eve* follows the account of Genesis 3 in viewing "labour" as a painful consequence of the fall:

> *The Life of Adam and Eve (Greek version) 24*[260]
> God said to Adam, "Seeing as you disobeyed my command and listened to your wife, the earth will be cursed in relation to your work. For when you work it, its strength will not give way. Thorns and thistles will grow up for you, and through the sweat of your face, you will eat your bread. There will be all sorts of toils: You will toil and not be refreshed. You will be crushed by bitterness and will not taste sweetness. You will be oppressed by heat and overwhelmed by cold. And you will labour much and not grow wealthy. And you will extend yourself without ever arriving at the goal. And the beasts, over which you ruled, will rise up against you in anarchy, because you did not keep my command."

Paul consistently refers to his apostolic activity in relation to the Corinthians as "work" or "labour" (arising from grace), and will end this climactic chapter by encouraging the Corinthians to adopt the same mindset, in view of the promise of future vindication (v58).

---

[260] This midrashic-style work expands on the account of Adam and Eve given in Genesis.

**15:12 But if it is proclaimed that Christ was raised from the dead, how is it that
some of you are saying that there is no resurrection of the dead? 13 If there is
no resurrection of the dead, neither was Christ raised. 14 And if Christ was
not raised, our proclamation is in vain, and your faith is in vain. 15 And we
have been found to be false witnesses of God, because we testified about
God that he raised Christ, whom he did not raise if in fact the dead are not
raised. 16 For if the dead are not raised, neither was Christ raised; 17 and if
Christ was not raised, your faith is useless, you are still in your sins, 18 and
accordingly those who have fallen asleep in Christ have perished. 19 If for
this life alone we have put our hope in Christ, we are to be pitied more than
all people.**

Some of you are saying that there is no resurrection of the dead
Acts 17:32 indicates that Athenian philosophers "scoffed" at the idea of resurrection. Paul's accusation here, however, is that *believers*, who do believe in the resurrection of Christ, are somehow denying the resurrection of dead believers. There are various reasons that people might claim that there is no resurrection of the dead – if indeed this may be read as a straightforward report of a propositional claim. Various possible backgrounds will be addressed in context below.

If for this life alone we have put our hope in Christ . . .
It seems that one of Paul's intentions in insisting on a future resurrection of the dead is *to resist the idea of the ultimacy of present existence*. Philo similarly seeks to contradict those "self-lovers" who reason that opportunities for power and wealth and bodily pleasures must be exploited in the present, because "the dead" cannot enjoy them:

> *Philo: The Worse Attacks the Better, 33*[261]
> [Self-lovers reason to themselves:] Isn't the body the house of the soul? Why then shouldn't we take care of the house, so that it will not become a ruin? Are not eyes and ears and the collection of other senses somewhat like bodyguards and friends of the soul? Should comrades and friends, then, not be held in the same honour as ourselves? But did nature create pleasures and enjoyments and all of the delights along the way of life, for the dead or for those never born, and not for those who are living? And wealth and glory and honour and rule and other such things – what will persuade us not to seek these things, which supply not only a safe life, but a happy life?

---

[261] Philo contrasts lovers of self (resembling Cain) with lovers of virtue (resembling Abel).

The *Wisdom of Solomon* similarly chides "the ungodly", whose observation that no one returns from death leads them to reason that they should be able to enjoy a dissolute life:

> *Wisdom of Solomon 1:12 . . . 15–2:1 . . . 6 . . . 21–22*[262]
> Do not seek death by the deception of your life.... For righteousness is immortal. But the ungodly, with their actions and their words, have called it upon themselves: Having considered it to be a friend, they have become dissolute and made an allegiance with it, because they are worthy to share in it. For they reasoned within themselves wrongly: "Our life is short and tedious, and there is no cure for the end of a person's life, and no one has been known to be released from Hades.... Come then and let us enjoy the good things that are here, and let us use creation to the full, as in youth".... These things they reasoned, and were deceived. For they were blinded by their own wickedness, and did not know the mysteries of God, or hope for the reward of holiness, or discern the prize for blameless souls.

2 Baruch 21:12–13 similarly considers that those who hope for "this life" alone are to be pitied.

15:20 But in fact Christ has been raised from the dead as the firstfruits of those who have fallen asleep. 21 For seeing as death came through a human, so the resurrection of the dead comes through a human. 22 For just as in Adam all died, so also in Christ all are brought to life. 23 But each in their own turn: Christ the firstfruits, then those who belong to Christ, at his coming.

As the firstfruits of those who have fallen asleep
The idea of the "firstfruits" of the harvest can be seen in Exodus 23; 34; Leviticus 2; and 23. There, it is an offering to God, whereas here it is an accomplishment by God.

Death came through a human
The assertion that death came through a "human" may recall the emphatic antithesis between "humanity" and "God" in chapters 1–4 (appearing again in 15:50).

The *Wisdom of Solomon* also carries the tradition that death "came" into the world, similarly drawing on Genesis 3 (cf. 4 Ezra 7:118; 2 Baruch 48:42):

---

262 This introduces a theme that will be prominent in the opening chapters of *Wisdom*: The juxtaposition of the boastful "ungodly" and the persecuted "righteous".

Wisdom of Solomon 2:23–24[263]
For God created humanity to be immortal, and he made them to be an image of his own eternity. But through the envy of the devil, death came into the world.

**15:24 And then the end comes, when he hands the kingdom to God the father,
when he brings to an end every rule and every authority and power. 25 For it is
necessary for him to reign until:**
All enemies are placed under his feet.
26 The final enemy to be brought down is death. For:
27 All things have been brought into subjection under his feet.
**But when it says that all things have been brought into subjection, it is plain
that this excludes the one who subjects all things to him. 28 But when all things
are brought into subjection to him, then the son himself will be subject to the
one who brought all things into subjection to him, in order that God might be
all in all.**

All enemies are placed under his feet; all things will be brought into subjection
Here Paul quotes Psalm 110:1 and Psalm 8:6. The Septuagint is largely followed, but is notably changed from second-person to third-person perspective. These two psalms are also combined in Ephesians 1:20–22 and Hebrews 2:5–8. The effect is to picture the risen Christ as the one who fulfils the divine vision for humanity.

Septuagint: Psalm 110:1 (numbered in the Septuagint as 109:1)
The Lord said to my lord, "Sit at my right hand, until your enemies are brought under your feet."

Daniel 7:13–14 similarly pictures a *human* receiving eternal dominion.

He brings an end to every rule and every authority and power
2 Maccabees exhibits the hope of those who die at the mercy of unjust rulers: The rulers will be brought down, and the righteous sufferers will receive resurrection:

2 Maccabees 7:7–9[264]
And after the first brother had died in this way, they led the second up for their mockery. And, having torn off the skin of his head with the hair,

[263] Wisdom is approaching the problem of the death of God's righteous people.
[264] This section depicts the martyrdoms of seven faithful brothers in defiance of an ungodly tyrant.

> they asked him, "Will you eat [unclean food] rather than have your body punished, one part at a time?" But he replied in the language of his father and said, "No". Therefore this brother also received mistreatment as had the first. And when he was at his last breath, he said, "You accursed wretch! You destroy our life in the present, but the king of the world will raise us up and give us eternal life, because we have died for his laws."
>
> *7:28–29*
> "I beg you, child: Look up to heaven and to the earth, and see everything that is in them, and know that God did not create them out of existing things – and so it is also with the human race. Do not fear this executioner, but be worthy of your brothers in also accepting death, in order that in His mercy, I might receive you back along with your brothers."
>
> *7:37–38*
> "And I, like my brothers, give both body and soul for the laws of the ancestors, calling upon God to be merciful soon to the nation, and with afflictions and plagues to make you [that is, the powerful unjust ruler] confess that there is one God, and through myself and my brothers to bring the wrath of the Almighty, which has been rightly brought upon our whole race, to a standstill."

Philo graphically exhibits the Jewish motif of divine reversal, as he pictures the death of Flaccus, who had persecuted the Jews, as the inevitable accomplishment of divine justice (cf. *On Providence*, 2.35–6):

> Philo: Flaccus, 189-91[265]
> With hands, feet, head, chest and ribs cut up, he lay there, sliced like a sacrificial victim, because Justice was willing to equal the number of his unlawful murders of the Jews with an equivalent number of butcheries in his one body. And the whole place was flooded with blood that poured out, gushing through many veins that were severed one by one. And as his dead body was being dragged into the pit that had been dug, most of the body parts came off, as the ligaments, which combine the whole body into one fellowship, had been torn apart. This was suffered by Flaccus, who thereby became indisputable confirmation that the Jewish nation has not been denied the protection that comes from God.

[265] This is the climactic ending of the work.

As noted above, Paul's application of this sort of motif here is not to particular people, but to "every rule and every authority and power" and death itself.

In order that God might be all in all
The glory of God has been an important implicit theme throughout the letter, as Paul has insisted that the Corinthians find their identity and status in God's Messiah rather than in Roman aspirations.

The *Book of the Watchers* looks ahead to the time when "all will be of God":

> *1 Enoch 1:8*[266]
> And they will all belong to God, and he will give them contentment, and he will bless all. And he will be the helper of all, and will aid us, and provide them with light, and bring peace upon them.

15:29 Or what are those people doing who are baptised on account of the dead?
If in fact the dead are not raised, why are they baptised on their account? 30 And
why are we badly treated every hour? 31 Every day I die, as surely as you are
my boast, brothers and sisters, which I have in Christ Jesus our Lord. 32 If for
human reasons I have fought wild beasts in Ephesus, what is the advantage to
me?

Baptised on account of the dead
Evidence for a practice of vicarious baptism in the first century is lacking. It may be that this is an ironic reference to the Corinthians' own squabbling (4:6) over baptism (1:13–17) in relation to metaphorically-dead apostles (4:9 and below, "Every day I die").[267]

Every day I die
Embracing death could be seen positively if it were a noble act of self-sacrifice; however Paul here envisages not a single act of gallantry, but an ongoing orientation.

Paul's stance is unlike that of Epictetus, who argues that the only reason death should be accepted ungrudgingly is because humans have no choice in the matter:

---

266 This verse forms part of the work's initial distinction between the destinies of the righteous and of sinners.

267 See Joel R. White, "'Baptised on Account of the Dead': The Meaning of 1 Corinthians 15:29 in its Context", *Journal of Biblical Literature*, 116/3 (1997), 487–499.

Epictetus: Discourse 1, 1.31–32 Concerning That Which is in Our Power and Not in Our Power[268]

It is necessary for me to die. If I must die now, then I will die now. And if after a little while, then I will come and eat now, and die afterwards. How? As one who gives up those things that belong to another.

Paul's implication is rather that he chooses to take on death, in the hope of future resurrection.

For human reasons

This phrase may hint at the distinction between that which is *human* and that which is ***divine***, established in chapters 1–4.

I have fought wild beasts in Ephesus

According to 16:8, the letter is written from Ephesus.

It may be that Paul's reference is to events described in Acts 19:28–9, where the Corinthian Gaius is mentioned alongside Paul (cf. 1 Corinthians 1:14) in an uprising at Ephesus. This is possibly the same event described in 2 Corinthians 1:8–11.

If the reference to "wild beasts" is not literal (as in Diodorus Siculus, 3.43.7), it may connote human or demonic opponents:[269] *Philo: Life of Moses, 1.43*[270]

> For some of the overseers were exceedingly wild and unconstrained, being no more tame than venomous and carnivorous animals, beasts in human shape, taking human bodily form in order that they might seem tame, only to hunt and catch their prey – because in reality they are harder than iron or steel.

Or perhaps the term connotes "personal passions":[271] Since the time of Plato, human passions had been likened to beasts that needed to be tamed:

---

[268] Epictetus is presenting the example of Agrippinus, who was unfazed by his trial at the Senate. He was able to maintain composure and perspective, because he remained clear about what was, and was not, in his own power.

[269] See, for example, Guy Williams, "An Apocalyptic and Magical Interpretation of Paul's 'Beast Fight' in Ephesus (1 Corinthians 15:32)" *The Journal of Theological Studies* 57/1 (2006), 42–56.

[270] Philo is picturing the overseers of the Hebrews during the time of their slavery in Egypt.

[271] See Abraham J. Malherbe, "The Beasts at Ephesus", *Journal of Biblical Literature* 87/1 (1968), 71–80.

Plato: Phaedrus 246a–b[272]

We will liken that which is innate to a pair of powerful winged horses and a charioteer. Now with regard to the gods, the horses and the charioteers are all good and of the good; but with regard to others, they are mixed. In our own case, the ruler holds the reins of the pair of horses. One is both good and noble and of this sort; but its opposite is indeed the antithesis. Thus our driving is, of necessity, difficult and troublesome.

It should be noted that the image brings the idea of "appointed death" to the foreground, as in 4:9.

The theatre at Ephesus (left):

Underneath the stage at the Colosseum in Rome, it is possible to see the passageways through which wild animals were brought up into the arena to fight:

15:32 **If the dead are not raised,**
Let us eat and drink, for tomorrow we die.
33 **Do not deceive yourselves:**
Bad company destroys good character.
34 **Sober up rightly and do not sin – for some of you possess ignorance of God! I say this to shame you.**

Let us eat and drink
Paul quotes from the Septuagint of Isaiah 22:13.

As earlier in the chapter, Paul here seems to be countering *a tendency to view the present as a time for making the most of indulgent pleasures*. Such a

---

272 This is Plato's famous image of the tripartite soul. The image of passions as "beasts" continued to be utilised in Greco-Roman philosophical reflection in the New Testament era.

tendency may betray an expectation that there is no afterlife, or an expectation that there is no *bodily* afterlife, or possibly the assumption that the feasting of the afterlife may begin in the present, without any concern for the future.

It is perhaps the first of these possible explanations that is illustrated in these tomb inscriptions recounted by Strabo:

> *Strabo: Geography, 14.5.9*[273]
> "Sardanapallus, child of Anakundaraxis, built Anchiale and Tarsus in one day. Eat, drink, play! – as all this is not worth it", meaning a snapping of the fingers. Choirilos also reminds of these things, and indeed these verses are well-travelled: "I have these things: As much as I have eaten and sown my wild oats and have felt the delights of love; but these many blessings I have left behind."

The *Epistle of Enoch* condemns those "sinners" who despise the dead and ridicule the possibility of their future vindication, and who choose to pursue merriment rather than faithful toil in the present:

> *1 Enoch 102:6–9*[274]
> When you died, then the sinners declared: "The godly died according to fate – and what did they gain from their works? They die just like us! See how they die with grief and darkness – what is the benefit to them? From this time, will they be raised, and will they be saved, and see into eternity? We eat and drink for this very reason, swindling and sinning and stealing and seizing property and seeing good days."

Bad company destroys good character
The quote is from Menander, but the entirety of its original context is not extant. It seems the saying had become proverbial by the time of 1 Corinthians.

15:35 But someone will say, "How will the dead be raised? With what sort of body will they come?" 36 Fool! You should know that the seed that you sow will

---

[273] These two proverbial sayings are presented as illustrative of the theme of the loss of all things at death.

[274] The "sinners" in the *Epistle of Enoch* are the rich, idolatrous, elite persecutors. At this point, the *Epistle* explores the respective experiences of the "sinners" and the "righteous" after death, ultimately concluding that the time will come when the sinners experience post-mortal condemnation and the righteous experience post-mortal vindication.

not come to life unless it dies; [37] and that which you sow is not the body that it will become, but a bare grain, whether of wheat or some other grain. [38] But God gives it a body according to his will – to each of the seeds its own body. [39] Not all flesh is the same, but there is one type for humans, one type of flesh for cattle, one type of flesh for birds, one type of flesh for fish. [40] And there are heavenly bodies and earthly bodies. But the glory of the heavenly is different to the glory of the earthly: [41] One type of glory for the sun, one type of glory for the moon, one type of glory for stars – for star differs from star in glory.

With what sort of body will they come?
Paul expects that some will object to his insistence on the future resurrection of the dead on the basis that *it is hard to fathom the revivification of bodies*. (2 Baruch 49:1–51:3 for a similar question about the nature of resurrection bodies.)

Greek and Roman views on the body, the soul, and the afterlife were diverse.

One important tradition, most famously associated with Plato, holds that death brings freedom for the immortal soul from the "prison" of the body:

> *Plato: Phaedrus 245e–246a*[275]
> But it is clear that that which moves of itself is immortal; and if one says that this is of the soul's being and logic, they will have no reason to be ashamed. For every body that is moved externally is soulless; but that which moves itself from within itself has a soul, as this is the nature of the soul. But if this is so – that nothing other than the soul moves itself – of necessity it must be permitted that the soul is both ungenerated and immortal.
>
> *246b–c*
> Being perfect and winged, it [the soul] flies and inhabits the whole world. But having shed its wings, it bears up until it takes hold of something solid, where it establishes itself, taking an earthly body, which itself seems to move because of that power. All together it is called a living being: soul and body together. It is designated as mortal; it is not for any reason to be considered immortal.

Epicurean and early Stoic philosophers rather argue that the soul is created along with the body, and is so intermingled with the body that it must also die along with the body:

---

[275] This and the subsequent citation flow from an argument about generation.

[276] This is part of an argument in which Epicurus suggests that the soul is diffused throughout the body, somewhat like breath or heat. The soul is so bound with the whole that it must dissipate when the whole disintegrates.

Epicurus: Epistle to Herodotus 67[276]
So those who say that the soul is incorporeal are speaking vainly.

Lucretius: 3.175–6[277]
Therefore the soul is necessarily of a corporeal nature, as it labours under the impact of corporeal spears.

3.275
Intermixed with our members and entire body is the power of the soul and of the spirit.

3.830
Death, therefore, is nothing to us – of no concern at all, if we understand that the soul has a mortal nature.

Plutarch: On Stoic Self-Contradictions 1053d[278]
And the proof he [the Stoic Chrysippus] uses that the soul is generated – and generated after the body – is mainly that the manner and character of the children bears a resemblance to their parents.

Sextus Empiricus: Against the Professors, 8.263[279]
For according to them [the Stoics] the incorporeal is not such that it can either act or suffer.

Other Stoics do seem to allow for the continued existence of the souls of the righteous (or indeed all souls) – until a final conflagration:

Eusebius: Evangelical Preparation, 15.20.6[280]
They [Stoics] say that the soul is both generated and mortal. But it is not immediately destroyed upon being separated from the body. Rather it remains for some time by itself – that of the diligent remains until the dissolution of all things by fire; and that of the foolish remains only for a limited time. About the endurance of the soul they say this: that we ourselves remain as souls which have been separated from the body and have

---

277 This is part of an argument in which Lucretius insists that both soul and spirit are constituted with a corporeal nature. Soul and body are so intertwined that they cannot be abstracted from each other.

278 Plutarch is attempting to show that Chrysippus is inconsistent.

279 This is part of a rebuttal of the Stoic theory of "sayables" (*lekta*).

280 Chapter 20 of this work explores what the Stoics (particularly Zeno) think about the soul.

been changed into the lesser substance of the soul; whereas the souls of irrational beings are destroyed along with their bodies.

Jewish views on the body, the soul, and the afterlife were also diverse. There are numerous resonances with the Platonic idea of an immortal soul that awaited liberation from its bodily prison:

Wisdom of Solomon 8:19–20[281]
I was a good child, receiving a good soul, or rather, being good, I came into an undefiled body.

Pseudo-Phocylides: Sentences, 105–108[282]
For souls remain unharmed in those who have perished. For the spirit is God's loan to mortals, and his image. For we have a body from the earth; and then after we are released to earth again, we are dust. But the air receives the spirit.

Sentences, 115
The soul is immortal and ageless, living forever.

Sentences 228[283]
Purifications are for the purity of the soul, rather than that of the body.

Josephus: Against Apion, 2.203[284]
For [in the act of sex] the soul is divided, departing to another place; for it suffers when being implanted in bodies and similarly at death when it is divided from them. Therefore purifications for all of these things are commanded.

Josephus: Jewish War, 2.154–155[285]
For this is their doctrine [that is, the Essenes]: That bodies are mortal, and their material is not permanent; but that souls are immortal and endure forever; and that they come out of thin air, so that they are bound to their bodies as to a prison, drawn in by a certain natural enticement; but being released from their fleshly bonds, as set free from a long slavery, they then

---

281 This expresses the experience of the one who seeks wisdom.

282 This and the subsequent citation occur within a section about death, grief, burial and the afterlife.

283 This is the start of the epilogue of the work, drawing its themes to a conclusion.

284 The context is a discussion of laws relating to marriage and purity.

285 Josephus is discussing the views of various sects within Judaism.

rejoice and rise upwards. And this is similar to the opinions of the Greeks who hold that good souls have a dwelling beyond the ocean.

The *Psalms of Solomon* appear to envisage a future resurrection "to eternal life" for the righteous, although it is not clear that this is definitely understood in bodily terms:

Psalms of Solomon 3:11–12[286]
The destruction of the sinner is forever
and such a person will not be remembered when God visits the righteous.
This is the fate of sinners forever;
but those who fear the Lord will be raised to eternal life.
And their life will be in the light of the Lord, and it will not go out.

But the idea of a future resurrection of bodies (or a future return to new bodies) was certainly prominent in early Judaism, probably arising from scriptural themes evident in Isaiah 26:19 and Daniel 12:1–3:

Josephus: Jewish War, 2.164[287]
[The Pharisees say that] every soul is immortal, but that only those of good people are removed into another body; while those of the simple are subjected to everlasting punishment.

Josephus: Jewish War, 3.372–74[288]
We all, indeed, have mortal bodies, and they are made up of perishable matter; but the soul is immortal forever.... Do you not know that those who depart from life in accordance with the law of nature, giving back the loan they had received from God, when the Giver wishes to reclaim it, receive eternal fame, and their houses and families are kept firm, and their souls remain pure and obedient, being assigned to the holiest place in heaven. From there, at the revolution of the ages, they return to inhabit sanctified bodies.

Josephus: Against Apion, 2.218[289]
To those who keep the laws, and if it is necessary to die for them, eagerly die, God has granted them to exist again, and a better life at the revolution [of the ages].

---

286 This psalm contrasts the righteous and sinners.
287 Josephus is discussing the views of various sects within Judaism.
288 Josephus is examining the ethics of suicide.
289 The focus of Josephus' point is the obedience of the law.

It is by no means certain, then, that those whom Paul addresses envisaged death as a welcome gateway to the liberation of an immortal soul. This was not an unquestioned assumption in Roman society.[290]

The seed that you sow will not come to life unless it dies
The mention of seeds, humans, animals, birds, fish, sun, moon, and stars suggests that the opening chapters of Genesis are in the background (coming to the foreground in the subsequent verses, which refer to Adam's creation from dust). God's work in resurrection is thus paralleled with God's work of creation.

It may be that the varying glory of "heavenly bodies", as created and ordered by the one God, undermines the Stoic interest in astrology, which was influential in the first century:

> *Stobaeus 1.213, 15–21*[291]
> Zeno says that the sun and the moon and the other stars are each intelligent and sensible, and possess a crafting sort of fire. For there are two types of fire, the one uncreative and self-feeding; the other creative, causing growth and maintenance – as can be seen in plants and animals, in which it is nature and soul. This sort of fire is the substance of the stars.

15:42 **So also it is with the resurrection of the dead. It is sown in perishability, it is raised in imperishability.**
43 **It is sown in dishonour, it is raised in glory. It is sown in weakness, it is raised in power.**
44 **It is sown a natural body, it is raised a Spiritual body. If there is a natural body, there is also a Spiritual body.**
45 **So it is written:**

The first human, Adam, became a natural being.
The last Adam became a life-giving Spirit.
46 **So the Spiritual does not come first, but the natural, then the Spiritual.**
47 **The first human was from the dust of the earth, the second human is from heaven.**
48 **As the one from earth, so those who are of the earth. As the one from heaven, so those who are of heaven.**
49 **And just as we have borne the image of the one from the earth, so also we will bear the image of the one from heaven.**

---

290 Indeed, Paul's initial response to the hypothetical objection about the body in verse 35 is to insist on the necessity of *death*. It may be that the central problem to which Paul responds in this chapter is an effective unwillingness to assume the role of the dead.

291 Stobaeus is portraying the thought of Zeno of Citium, the founder of Stoicism. For similar terminology to Paul from a Jewish perspective, see Sirach 43:1–10.

It is sown in dishonour, it is raised in glory
The mention of "dishonour" reminds of the use of this provocative terminology throughout the letter to refer to those in the apostolic mould (cf. especially 4:10).

Daniel 12:1–4 also uses the imagery of stars, heaven, and glory to speak of the expected resurrection of those who presently sleep in dust. See also 1 Enoch 62:15; 105:11–12.

The first human, Adam, became a natural being
This is a quotation of Genesis 2:7, in which the Septuagint's "man" has been further specified as "the first man, Adam". The passage is quoted to support the idea that the "spiritual" body is a necessary sequel to the "natural". The point seems to be that those who belong to Christ, being still chiefly characterised by their natural bodies, await the time when they will be *utterly* animated and energised by the Spirit of Jesus Christ.

> *Septuagint: Genesis 2:7*
> And God moulded the man out of dust from the earth, and breathed the breath of life into his face, and the man became a living being [ψυχὴν ζῶσαν].

Philo also quotes this verse. His purpose, however, is to point out a distinction between body and soul:

> *Philo: Allegorical Interpretation, 3.161*[292]
> The body was formed out of the earth; but the soul is of the atmosphere, a divine particle: "For God breathed the breath of life into his face, and the man became a living soul [ψυχὴν ζῶσαν]."

Daniel 12:2–3 similarly looks ahead to the resurrection of those who sleep in the dust of the earth.

The idea that God's power in *creation* is parallel to his activity in *resurrection* is not new with Paul. Psalm 104:27–30; Isaiah 44:2, 24; *2 Maccabees* 7:28–29; and 2 Esdras 6:6 all link God's work of creation with his power to raise to new life:

---

[292] In context, Philo is making a distinction between types of food: The soul eats "heavenly" food (knowledge), while the body requires earthly food.

2 Maccabees 7:28–29[293]
"I beg you, child: Look up to heaven and to the earth, and see everything that is in them, and know that God did not create them out of existing things – and so it is also with the human race. Do not fear this executioner, but be worthy of your brothers in also accepting death, in order that in His mercy, I might receive you back along with your brothers."

As we have borne the image of the one from the earth
Philo distinguishes between the heavenly man and the fallen earthly man of Genesis 1–2:

Philo: Allegorical Interpretation, 3.252[294]
For is he not now classed among the earthly and chaotic, having abandoned heavenly wisdom?.... But perhaps what he is saying is like this: The foolish mind has always turned away from the right principle, and comes not from the heavenly nature, but from the more earthly matter.

15:50 Now this is what I am saying, brothers and sisters: That flesh and blood cannot inherit the kingdom of God, and the perishable cannot inherit the imperishable. 51 See, I am telling you a mystery: We will not all sleep, but we will all be changed, 52 in a moment, in the twinkling of an eye, at the last trumpet.

Flesh and blood
This idiom is used elsewhere by Paul to refer to humans – as opposed to super-human beings: See Galatians 1:16, Ephesians 6:12 (cf. Matthew 16:17). To say that "flesh and blood cannot inherit the kingdom of God" might thus be parallel to saying, "No more boasting in *humans*"; "Let the one who boasts boast in the *Lord*" (3:21; 1:31).

I am telling you a mystery
Paul has spoken about his role as an apostle as a "steward of the mysteries of God" in chapters 1–4. The idea of sharing a "mystery" reminds of Israel's wisdom tradition, in which God reveals his purposes to those who trust him. The *Epistle of Enoch*, for example, similarly speaks about the vindication of the righteous dead as a "mystery" which God has revealed:

---

293 The mother of seven sons is here urging them to face martyrdom bravely, in expectation of future resurrection.

294 This is part of a discussion of the curse of the fall in Genesis 3:18.

1 Enoch: 103:1–3[295]
I swear to you.... I understand this mystery…. That goodness and joy and honour have been prepared and written down for the souls of those who have died while godly.

15:52 For the trumpet will blast and the dead will be raised imperishably, and we will be changed. 53 For it is necessary for this perishability to be clothed with imperishability and for this mortality to be clothed with immortality.

The trumpet will blast
The theme of the Day of the Lord beginning with the blast of a trumpet appears in Isaiah 27:13; Joel 2:1; and Zephaniah 1:16. See also 4 Ezra 6:23, Apocalypse of Moses 22, 27, and Apocalypse of Abraham 31:1–2.

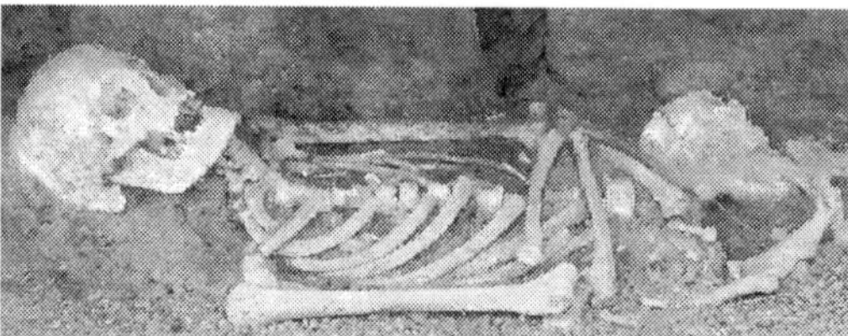

The dead will be raised
Left is an early Christian burial at Nemea, which is near Corinth. The head is raised, facing the East, in expectation of resurrection at the return of Christ.

It is necessary for this mortality to be clothed with immortality
It seems that one of Paul's intentions in insisting on a future resurrection of the dead is *to affirm that immortality can only be received as a future gift from God.*

It may be that Christian ideas of present triumph had combined with other philosophical notions of present immortality in Corinth. Epicurus, and following him, the Epicurean school, denounced the plight of the dead, but were able to describe their own present lives as, in some sense, "immortal" and "divine":

Epicurus: Letter to Menoeceus, 123[296]
Firstly, think of God as an imperishable and blessed being.

125
Therefore death, the most fearsome of evils, is nothing to us, seeing as when we exist, death is not present; and when death is present, we do not exist.

[295] This comes at the end of the *Epistle of Enoch,* where the destinies of the righteous and of sinners are contrasted.

[296] This follows the introduction of the letter. In context, Epicurus is affirming the existence of gods, but denying that the masses have understood the gods rightly.

So death is nothing to those who are living or to those who have died, seeing as for the one, *it* is nothing, and for the other, *they* are nothing.

135
But you [the follower of Epicurus' ways] will live as a god among humans. For a person living amidst immortal virtues is nothing like a mortal being.

Plutarch: Against Epicurean Happiness, 1091b–c[297]
What great pleasure belongs to these people [the Epicureans], and what blessing they enjoy, rejoicing about their lack of suffering and grief and pain! Therefore, is it not fitting, on account of these things, also to think and to speak as they do speak, calling themselves imperishable and equal to gods…!

Philo views Moses as having entered into immortality, from which state he offers unrestrained spiritual prophecy. He elsewhere indicates that in some sense, the *wise* person lives an immortal or divine life, while the wayward person experiences death in this life. Philo thus combines Jewish terminology and values (such as monotheism) with certain conceptions and assumptions of contemporary philosophy (such as conceptions of immortality and indestructibility). Perhaps something similar was occurring in Corinth, as believers sought to interpret their new life in Christ as including some sort of inaugurated immortality.

Philo: Life of Moses, 2.288[298]
But later, the time came when he had to journey from this habitation to heaven, and to leave mortal life to become immortal, having been called by the Father, who transformed his dual nature, body and soul, into a single nature, converting his whole self into sun-like mind. Then, indeed, he was no longer restrained to prophesy collectively to the whole nation as a group together, but now also was able to prophesy part by part, to each tribe, concerning the things that were to come, and must come to pass.

Philo: The Worse Attacks the Better, 48–49[299]
For the soul from which the love of virtue and love of God have been removed has died to the life of virtue.… So then, the wise person, who

297 Plutarch is arguing against the Epicurean characterisation of "good" in negative terms.

298 This comes at the end of the work, and illustrates a number of Philo's values: immortality; purity of mind; spiritual prophecy.

299 Philo is drawing a principle from the fact that Abel's blood is said to "speak" after he is dead.

seems to die to mortal life, lives the immortal life. But the worthless person, who lives in wickedness, dies to happiness.

Philo: On Dreams, 2.253[300]
Whoever, then, has the strength to leave behind war and fate, creation and mortality, and cross over to the uncreated, to the immortal, to free will, and to peace, might rightly be said to be the dwelling-place and city of God.

Philo: Every Good Man is Free, 43:
[According to the philosophy of Moses,] the one who possesses love for the divine and worships the one Being is no longer human, but has become a god – but a god in relation to humans, not in relation to all parts of nature, so that in relation to all "gods", the Father is left to be king and God.

Paul rather wishes to emphasise that the full experience of wisdom, immortality and communion with God is deferred to the time of the appearance of Christ.

2 Baruch 50–51 similarly insists that those who enter glory must be changed.

This perishability . . . this mortality
The two terms are frequently used in parallel, as in the *Wisdom of Solomon* (cf. Philo, *The Eternity of the World*, 19):

Wisdom of Solomon 9:13–15[301]
For what human can know the counsel of God? Or who can discern what the Lord wills? For the reasonings of *mortals* are worthless, and our understanding fails. For a *perishable* body weighs down the soul, and an earthly dwelling weighs down the thinking mind.

15:54 And when this perishability is clothed with imperishability, and this mortality is clothed with immortality, then that which is written will come about:
Death is consumed by victory.
55 Where, O Death, is your victory?
Where, O Death, is your sting?
56 The sting of death is sin, and the power of sin is the law. 57 But thanks be to God, who gives us the victory through our Lord Jesus Christ.

---

300 Philo's point in context is that "coming to peace" is effectively the same as "coming to God", as God is the one who truly embodies peace and immortality.

301 In context, this section is emphasising the necessity of divine wisdom.

Death is consumed by victory
This is a quotation of Isaiah 25:8, although it differs significantly from the Septuagint. The effect of this quotation is to emphasise the unity of the themes of resurrection and salvation: Salvation of God's people (the theme of Isaiah 25) will only have been completed when death has been conquered by resurrection.

> *Septuagint: Isaiah 25:8*
> Death, victorious, has consumed; but again, God has taken every tear from every face.

Where, O Death, is your victory?
This is a quotation of Hosea 13:14. Paul's rendering differs from both the Hebrew and the Septuagint. Paul's use of this verse is ironic: For Hosea, it was a summons for death to enact its judgement; for Paul, it is a pointed announcement of the judgement that has come upon death itself.

> *Septuagint: Hosea 13:14*
> Out of the hand of Hades I will rescue them, and out of death I will redeem them. Where is your punishment, Death? Where is your sting, Hades?

The book of *Sirach* addresses death as a foe for the contented, and a merciful end for the despairing:

> *Sirach: 41:1–3*[302]
> O Death, how bitter is the thought of you to a person living at peace among their possessions, to one who is free of distractions and blessed in all things, and still strong enough to partake in food!
> O Death, how good your judgement is to the person who is needy and who lacks strength; to the one who is in old age, and is beset by all sorts of distractions, and who despairs, and who has lost endurance.
> Do not fear the judgement of death: Remember those who have come before you, and those who will come later: This is the judgement of the Lord on all flesh.

The *Testament of Abraham* presents "Death" as a figure subject to God's rule:

---

[302] This occurs after an exhortation to be contented rather than a beggar.

Testament of Abraham: Recension A, 16.1–9[303]
Then the Most High said, "Call here to me Death, the one who is called the shameless face and the unmerciful glance."
And Michael the incorporeal one went to Death and said, "Come! The master of creation, the immortal king, calls you."
And hearing this, Death shivered and trembled, being overcome with great terror. And coming with great fear, he stood before the invisible Father, shivering, moaning and trembling, desperately waiting for the command of the master.

Thanks be to God
Here Paul seems to reword a common phrase, to make it monotheistic:

Oxyrhynchus papyrus 113.13 (2nd century CE*)*
Thanks be to the gods.

Praising God for his victory is an important feature of the Jewish motif of reversal (e.g. the Song of Moses in Exodus 15; the song of Hannah in 1 Samuel 2; the song of Deborah in Judges 5; the song of Mary in Luke 1). The *Prayer of Azariah* repeatedly praises God for saving the "three Jews" from Hades:

Prayer of Azariah 1.88[304]
Bless the Lord, Hananiah, Azariah and Mishael; sing and highly exalt him forever, because he has taken us out of Hades, and saved us from the hand of Death, and rescued us from the midst of the flaming furnace, and freed us from the fire!

15:58 **So, my beloved brothers and sisters, stand firm, immovable, always abounding in the work of the Lord, knowing that your labour is not in vain in the Lord.**

---

303 Death is here depicted as a cowering figure under God's command. He is commanded to take Abraham.

304 This is the climax of this single-chapter addition to the book of Daniel.

Those Who Labour

**[16:1] Now concerning the collection for the saints: You should act in accordance
with the directions I gave to the churches of Galatia. [2] On the first day of the
week, each of you should put aside an amount at home, according to your own
prosperity, so that when I come, the collection will not need to be made. [3] But
when I do arrive, I will send those you approve, with letters of recommendation, to Jerusalem, along with your gift. [4] And if it seems fitting that I should
go too, they will go with me.**

Put aside an amount at home, according to your own prosperity
Leviticus 25:35–6 calls the people of God to care for fellow Israelites who have become unable to support themselves. Numbers 18:23–4 explains that the Levites are to be provided for by the tithes of the rest of the Israelites. Deuteronomy 15:1–18 encourages the people of Israel to share the blessings of God's provision with the poor and with freed slaves.

With letters of recommendation
A papyrus letter of recommendation from about 25 CE:

> *Oxyrhynchus papyrus 292 (25 CE)*
> Theon, to the honourable Tyrannus: Many greetings! Herakleides, the one bringing this letter to you, is my brother. Therefore I urge you with all of my power to bring him into your company. I have also asked Hermias the brother, via letter, to tell you about him. You will be doing me the greatest act of kindness if you will take note of him. Above all, I pray that you might have health, be free from harm, and do well. Goodbye.

**[16:5] Now, I will come to you when I have gone through Macedonia. For I am going
through Macedonia, [6] and it may happen that I will stay with you or even spend
the winter, so that you might send me on my way, wherever I may go. [7] For I do
not want to see you now in passing – for I hope to spend some time with you if
the Lord permits it. [8] So I will remain in Ephesus until Pentecost, [9] for a great and
productive door has opened for me, and there are many opponents.**

Spend the winter
Travel was limited during the winter, as ships did not normally travel, due to the dangerous conditions. See Acts 20:3, 6; 28:11; 2 Timothy 4:21; Titus 3:12.

**16:10 But if Timothy does come, watch that he has nothing to fear while with you.
For he works as I do in the work of the Lord. 11 Let no one treat him with contempt, but send him on in peace, in order that he might come to me. For I am
waiting for him with the brothers.**

**12 Now concerning Apollos the brother: I strongly urged him to come to you
with the brothers, and he was entirely unwilling to come now; but he will
come when he has an opportunity.**
**13 Be watchful, stand firm in the faith, be courageous, be strong. 14 Let every-
thing you do happen in accordance with love.**

**15 Now I appeal to you, brothers and sisters: You know the household of
Stephanas, that they were the firstfruits of Achaia, and set themselves aside
for service to the saints. 16 I urge you to obey people such as these, and all
those who work together and labour. 17 I rejoice at the coming of Stephanas
and Fortunatus and Achaicus, because they filled what was lacking from you,
18 for they refreshed my spirit and yours. Give recognition to people such as
these.**

Give recognition
It seems that the Corinthians were failing to adequately honour local leaders, while squabbling about external figureheads (see 1:10–17). Paul has attempted to attack the fundamental theological problem of "boasting in humans" that underlies this behaviour (1:31; 3:21). He now seeks to restore honour to those who "labour" by following the apostolic imitation of Christ's death (see 3:8, 13–15; 4:12; 9:1; 15:10, 58).

The command to "give recognition" thus differs from conventional Roman values not in terminology, but in the transformed concept of what is truly praiseworthy: *Christ-imitating, God-dependent cruciform labour*.

**16:19 The churches of Asia greet you. Aquila and Prisca greet you warmly in the
Lord, together with the church that meets in their house. 20 All of the brothers
and sisters greet you. Greet one another with a holy kiss.**

The churches of Asia greet you.
Ephesus was in the Roman province of Asia (see opposite):

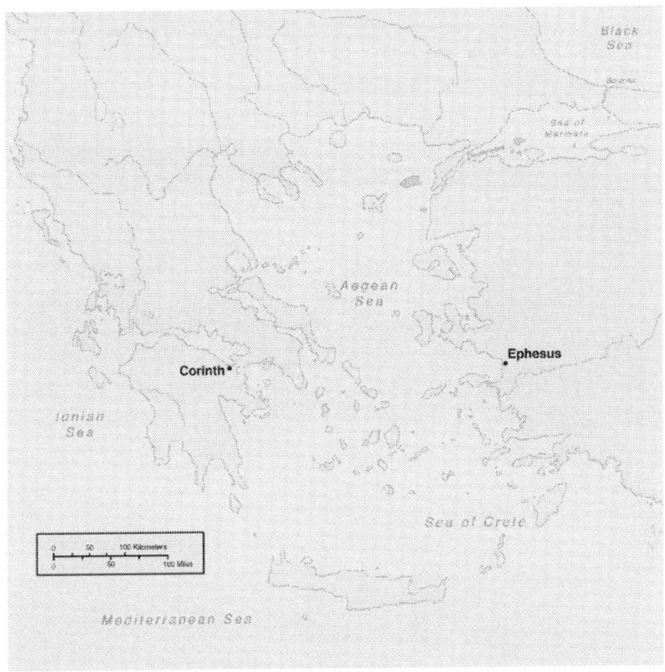

16:21 This greeting is in my own handwriting – Paul's. 22 If anyone does not love
the Lord, let them be accursed. Maranatha! 23 The grace of the Lord Jesus be
with you. 24 My love to all of you in Christ Jesus. Amen.

My own handwriting

Letters were often written by a professional letter-writer or secretary, with the content confirmed by a brief summary or signature in the handwriting of the actual author.

The following written agreement follows the same pattern: the details of the contract are elucidated in the main body, followed by a confirmation in different handwriting. In this situation, it appears that the author was illiterate, and so had a family member write the confirmation. The confirmation appears below:

> Papyrus letter (99CE)
> I, Thenetkouis of Heron, Persian, with my custodian and relative Leontas of Hippalus, acknowledge that I have from Lucius the initial payment of 16 silver drachmas, and I will work at the olive press from whatever day you give me the order, receiving from you, Lucius, wages that match that of similar workers, and I will do each thing just as it has

been said above. Leontas has written this also on behalf of Thenektouis, who is not literate.

Maranatha!
This is a transliteration of an Aramaic phrase that no doubt came to Paul from the early Aramaic speaking Christians, meaning, "Come, Lord!"

Biblical Index

Made in the USA
Middletown, DE
04 October 2022